CW00666353

The Blitz
IN COLOUR

Warners Group Publications
The Maltings
West Street
Bourne
Lincolnshire
PE10 9PH
Tel: 01778 391000
Fax: 01778 392422
www.warnersgroup.co.uk

Publisher
Rob McDonnell
robm@warnersgroup.co.uk
Editor
Andy Saunders
andy.saunders@warnersgroup.co.uk
Tel: 01753 770712

DESIGN
Head of Design and Production
Lynn Wright
Designer
Mike Edwards

MARKETING
Marketing Manager
Katherine Brown
katherine.brown@warnersgroup.co.uk
Tel: 01778 395092
Marketing Executive
Luke Hider
luke.hider@warnersgroup.co.uk
Tel: 01778 395085

ADVERTISING
Sales Executive
Kristina Green
kristina.green@warnersgroup.co.uk
Tel: 01778 392096

PRODUCTION
Production Manager
Nicola Glossop
nicola.glossop@warnersgroup.co.uk
Tel: 01778 392420
Production Assistant
Charlotte Bamford
charlotte.bamford@warnersgroup.co.uk
Tel: 01778 395081

DISTRIBUTION
Warners Distribution
Andy Perry
Tel: 01778 391152

This publication is printed by Warners
01778 395111

Welcome

The Blitz is an event in British military history which will forever remain embedded in the collective national consciousness. And, however doubtful the value or relevance of such a term might be in the 21st Century, the expression 'Blitz Spirit' has endured across the 80 years since the Blitz to suggest a spirit of resilience in the face of hardship and adversity. However inappropriate its application might have been to any event suffered nationally across subsequent decades, the fact that the expression is very much part of the English lexicon - and something which is universally understood – speaks volumes as to the impact that the events of the Blitz had upon the British psyche.

With the word's origins attached to the German word 'Blitzkrieg' (meaning Lightning War), the single term Blitz has evolved to be understood as the bombing of British cities by the Luftwaffe. Primarily, of course, the Blitz is associated with the German air assault on London between September 1940 and May 1941. However, it is important to recognise that the Blitz involved the majority of British cities: including Glasgow, Belfast, Southampton, Bristol, Coventry and Birmingham. That list, though, is not in any way exhaustive. It is also the case that a huge number of other towns and villages came in for attention by the Luftwaffe across almost the entire duration of the war, and not just the period of the September 1940 to May 1941 Blitz. Additionally, the nation was also attacked from the air and from the sea during the First World War, too.

In this publication, then, we have looked at the whole range and scope of attacks against the entirety of the British Isles (including the First World War) which largely targeted the civilian population and industrial or non-military objectives. During the Second World War, this also includes the devastating Tip and Run attacks against largely coastal towns as well as the fearsome V1 Flying Bomb and V2 rocket attacks.

Throughout the Second World War alone, a total of 60,595 civilians were killed as the result of air attacks. Putting this figure into perspective against Britain's total number of military fatalities during the war (376,239) it represents around 16% of that total.

While the very largest percentage of those civilian casualties were suffered in the big towns or cities, it is hard to find a single rural community across mainland Britain which did not suffer a fatality or casualty. Thus, the Blitz on Britain affected almost every single community. And the whole nation was on the front line. Or potentially so.

In this publication to mark the 80th anniversary of the main part of the Blitz, we have looked at a wide range of related topics, examined how Britain was defended, how it was attacked and how the civilian population withstood an extraordinary assault.

In compiling this record of the varied attacks on Britain, we have examined that period through a range of colour images, including photographs that have been colourised specifically for this publication.

We hope that you enjoy this unique look at one of the most dramatic periods in Britain's recent history.

This publication is dedicated to the memory of the 60,595 innocent civilian lives so cruelly taken during the nation's dreadful ordeal under fire.

Andy Saunders
Editor, The Blitz in Colour

CONTENTS

The Blitz IN COLOUR

INSIDE THIS COMMEMORATIVE PUBLICATION

CONTENTS

CONTRIBUTORS

Richard J Molloy
The colourisation artist for this project was Richard J Molloy who specialises in the digital colourisation of historic images. His particular interest is with military subjects and he is a regular art contributor to Iron Cross magazine, also by Warners Group Publications Plc.

Using research based on known colours, and sometimes using period colour charts, Richard constructs accurate representations of period images. His evaluation of those images often requires forensic research to properly represent the image being coloured.

This piece of work on the Blitz on Britain is Richard's second such project for Warners Group Publications Plc, his first being Battle of Britain in Colour published in 2020. Samples of Richard J Molloy's work may be viewed by searching:- @colourbyRJM

Andy Godfrey
The aircraft colour profile artwork for this publication was by Andy Godfrey of the Teasel Studio.

Andy specialises in bespoke profile artworks for publication and commission.

Working from his studio near Hastings, East Sussex, his work draws on an extensive reference collection, gathered over five decades, a deep fascination with aircraft and specialist knowledge of colours and markings. For enquiries:- teaselstudio@yahoo.co.uk

Acknowledgements
The editor wishes to thank Ian Castle, Austin J Ruddy and Steve Hunnisett for their individual and valuable contributions to this publication.

Cover Story Focke-Wulf 190 fighter-bombers streak away from Eastbourne on 4 June 1943 after one of the devastating tip-and-run attacks endured by the town.
Artwork by Piotr Forkasiewicz

'No Longer an Island'

At the dawn of the 20th century, Britons slept soundly in their beds, safe in the knowledge that the Royal Navy protected the coastline from enemy aggression. However, advances in aeronautics soon exposed the country to assault from the air.

In July 1900, a retired German Army officer, Count Ferdinand von Zeppelin, launched his first eponymous airship using lighter-than-air gas, hydrogen, to lift its great bulk into the sky. Over the next years, von Zeppelin continued to experiment and by 1910 Zeppelins were operating regular flights over Germany. It was a fact not underestimated by the German military.

Six years later, aeroplane development had progressed slowly in comparison to airships, and when an aviation pioneer claimed a prize for being the first to complete a flight of over 100 metres in 1906 there was little reaction. However, a newspaper baron, Lord Northcliffe, recognised its stark significance, remarking:

'England is no longer an island.'

Despite this early warning, Britain had little in the way of air defence when the country declared war on Germany in August 1914.

HATRED FOR GERMANY

At that time, the Army and Royal Navy each had an air arm, the Royal Flying Corps (RFC) and the Royal Naval Air Service (RNAS). When the RFC accompanied the British Expeditionary Force to the battlefields of Europe, the RNAS accepted responsibility – temporarily – to defend Britain against aerial attack. Other than a diverse collection of 50 seaplanes and landplanes, there were just a handful of efficient anti-aircraft guns defending military installations. London only received its first guns – three ineffective one pounders – four days after the declaration of war.

There had never been a sustained aerial bombing campaign before and nobody could be sure what impact bombs falling amongst the civilian population would have on morale. In Germany, as early as August 1914, Paul Behncke, Deputy Chief of the Naval Staff, expressed his belief that attacks on London were likely:

'...to cause panic in the population which may possibly render it doubtful that the war can be continued.'

Later, in October 1914, he warmed to his subject:

'We dare not leave untried any means of forcing England to her knees, and successful air attacks on London, considering the well-known nervousness of the public, will be a valuable measure.'

10772 IB
THE GERMAN AIR RAID ON GREAT YARMOUTH, JANUARY 19th, 1915.
MR. ELLIS WOUNDED BY A BOMB, AND HIS RUINED HOUSE, AT LANCASTER ROAD CORNER,
ST. PETER'S PLAIN.

Facing Page Ground personnel load 50kg bombs onto a Gotha G V, preparatory to an air raid against Britain.

Above Bomb damage in Great Yarmouth during the first Zeppelin raid on Britain. The bomb that wrecked this house in St. Peter's Plain also claimed the lives of the first two people in Britain killed by a bomb dropped from the air: Samuel Smith (aged 53) and Martha Taylor (72).

He was wrong. When bombs did start to fall across Britain there was no crumbling of morale but instead a hatred for Germany as its bombs killed innocent civilians as they lay asleep in their beds. And anger, too, that the British military appeared, initially at least, to have no effective means to oppose the raids.

AWE AND WONDER

The first significant raid took place in January 1915, when two Zeppelins bombed Great Yarmouth, King's Lynn and a number of Norfolk villages, claiming the lives of four and injuring 16 others. Something that seemed impossible just a few years earlier had become reality. And when those first bombs exploded, they opened-up a whole new theatre of war: The Home Front.

The experiences of those on the ground living through the raids varied enormously. Many people in Britain had not even seen an aeroplane before the war, and so when one of these huge airships passed over the blacked-out towns, cities and villages, illuminated by searchlights while moving serenely

on, they aroused widespread awe and wonder. Others, meanwhile, were simply – and understandably - terrified.

Air raid warnings were left to the discretion of local authorities and where such arrangements existed, they took the form of hooters or whistles sounded at factories or by the raising and lowering of gas pressure, which changed the brightness of lights in homes and workplaces. In London, though, there was no air raid warning system. Although debated, the government concluded

Top For residents of Britain during the First World War, the Zeppelin was an object of awe, wonder and fear.

Above Left In 1915, German airships attacking Britain had it more-or-less their own way as air defences only slowly developed. In 1916, however, the advantage swung back in favour of the defenders.

Above Right The demise of Schütte-Lanz SL 11 in September 1916, the first airship shot down over mainland Britain, spawned numerous lurid postcards. This one carried the title: 'Death of the Baby-Killer'.

'If we can suppose that they had really some definite objective other than the mere haphazard destruction of the lives and property of non-combatants, then, owing to the height at which they flew, they entirely failed to attain that objective. Of the 127 persons killed or injured, none, save one or two soldiers who were in the street at the time, were combatants.'

British Government Statement, October 1915.

that by sounding a warning it would encourage people to congregate in the streets to watch, risking their own safety and obstructing emergency services - a genuine problem.

'BLITZ SPIRIT'

Zeppelins generally only attacked singly with their course easy to follow if weather conditions permitted. And while it was terrifying for those who found themselves in the Zeppelin's path, for others only a short distance away the same experience could be an exciting and thrilling one. Shortly after any raid, great crowds would descend on the bombed area to view the damage and often to be photographed standing in craters. And there was another reaction never anticipated in Germany: the British public bought 'comic' postcards that made jokes of the raids to send to family and friends in an early example of the 'Blitz Spirit' we commonly associate with the next war.

Throughout 1915, German airships raided Britain on 20 separate occasions, attacking London five times, with others targeting places such as Hull, Southend-on-Sea, Jarrow and Goole, but not venturing too far inland if possible. During this time, the Zeppelins more-or-less had it their own way, with Britain's defences offering little in the way of opposition. In one raid on London on the night of 8/9 September 1915, the bombs dropped by a lone Zeppelin as it passed over the centre of the city caused damage with an estimated value of over half a million pounds. It was the most costly of any air raid throughout the war.

The Zeppelins that raided Britain in the second half of 1915 were giants in comparison with Count Zeppelin's first airship, measuring 163.5 metres in length

Looking for Zeppelins at WOOLWICH

with a capacity of 31,900 cubic metres of hydrogen. But a new type in service in the latter half of 1916 took on even greater dimensions, attaining a length of 197 metres and containing an incredible 55,200 cubic metres of hydrogen. More hydrogen meant the airship could carry a greater weight of bombs.

VICTORIA CROSS

It would seem likely that a target this big, holding such a colossal amount of a highly inflammable gas, should be simple to find and destroy. But that was not the case. Zeppelin raids followed the cycle of the moon, only taking place on the darkest nights of each month. And even when found, the difficulties did not end there. Hydrogen only becomes flammable when mixed with oxygen, but inside the bulk of a Zeppelin the gas was contained in a number of gas-

tight bags. Lead bullets fired into them would only make tiny holes without any means of igniting the slowly escaping gas. The ponderous Home Defence aircraft carried bombs or explosive darts to drop on the Zeppelin, but they could not match an airship's ability to climb rapidly away from danger. More anti-aircraft guns were becoming available, but it was difficult to gauge the range with accuracy in the relatively short periods the target remained in view while searchlights battled to hold them.

German airships appeared in far greater numbers over Britain on the 22 nights they raided in 1916, penetrating much deeper into the country than before with attacks on the industrial North, the Midlands and into Scotland. A raid on the Midlands on the night of 31 January exposed the lack of defences there, with nine Zeppelins roaming at

Deutsches Riesen-Flugzeug
(Englandflieger)

will entirely unopposed. Their bombs killed 72 and injured over a hundred. In February 1916, however, responsibility for Home Defence passed from the Admiralty to the War Office and major changes saw an improvement in the efficiency of the country's air raid response. And behind the scenes, work was underway to give pilots the weapon they needed to end the Zeppelin menace: new bullets, explosive and incendiary.

In the autumn of 1916 these bullets claimed their first victim when a RFC pilot, William Leefe Robinson, shot down an airship in the early hours of 3 September, the explosive bullets bursting open a gas bag to release the hydrogen and an incendiary bullet igniting the now volatile gas. For his actions that night, Leefe Robinson was awarded the Victoria Cross.

The bullets claimed two more Zeppelins within four weeks, and a combination of anti-aircraft fire and bullets forced another down intact. Then in November, pilots shot down two more.

AIR RAID WARNING SYSTEM

In 1917, Zeppelins raided on only six nights and in 1918 that reduced even further to just three. The threat of air raids, however, did not diminish and from May 1917 Germany launched a

Top Powered by two 260hp Mercedes engines, the 78-foot wingspan Gotha could maintain a speed of 80mph in favourable conditions, carrying a three-man crew, two or three machine guns and a bomb load of between 300 and 400kgs.
Above Right The types of P.u.W. aerial bombs available to German bomber aeroplanes in 1918. From left to right: 50kg, 100kg, 300kg and 1,1000kg, while the man in the centre holds a 12.5kg bomb.
Above Left This painting by Ronald Gray depicts RNAS gunners at London's Cannon Street anti-aircraft station during 1917. Searchlights probe the sky for Zeppelins or bombers.
Facing Page Top During the Zeppelin phase of the war, crowds of people visited bombed areas, many posing for photographs in craters. These enthusiastic bomb-seekers gathered in the north-east of England in 1915.
Facing Page Below An example of one of the many comic postcards produced during the period of Zeppelin attacks on Britain.

IT IS FAR BETTER
TO FACE THE BULLETS
THAN TO BE KILLED
AT HOME BY A BOMB

JOIN THE ARMY AT ONCE
& HELP TO STOP AN AIR RAID

GOD SAVE THE KING

Above The message of this Army recruitment poster turned the Zeppelin raids to advantage.
Right On London's Embankment, a bomb dropped by a Gotha damaged Cleopatra's Needle and its flanking Sphynx guardians. A gas main was ruptured and the driver and two passengers on a passing tram were killed. Splinter marks from the blast can still be seen today – tangible evidence of London's first Blitz.

new aeroplane against Britain, the Grosskampfflugzeug, better known as the Gotha bomber.

After an attack on Folkestone on 25 May, when a bomb killed 61 people queuing outside a greengrocers' shop, a squadron of Gothas attacked London on 13 June. It was the first raid on the capital for eight months, and the first in broad daylight. The casualties were the highest of any raid in the war: 162 killed and 426 injured. Amongst the dead were 18 children killed at school, the majority just five years old. The public were outraged, and serious outbreaks of anti-German rioting occurred.

After another daylight raid on 7 July, London finally got an air raid warning system, two years after the first attack on the capital. The system, however, was a far cry from the wailing sirens of the Second World War. It involved policemen touring the streets with placards bearing the words, 'Police Notice - Take Cover', while they blew whistles, rung bells or sounded horns to attract attention.

Those first Gotha raids resulted in an urgent review of London's defences and

led to the creation of the London Air Defence Area (L.A.D.A.) uniting all the separate elements, the aeroplanes, guns, searchlights and observers, all under a single command.

INTENSE PERIOD OF BOMBING

With losses amongst raiding Gothas increasing as the summer wore on, it led to a switch to night bombing, but with London at the Gotha's extreme range, so the rest of the country to the north of the capital was free from their attentions. More advanced aircraft now began to bolster Home Defence squadrons and new schemes to concentrate anti-aircraft fire on fixed points made life increasingly dangerous for the Gotha crews.

In the autumn of 1917, a new aircraft joined the Gothas, the massive Riesenflugzeug, literally: 'Giant aeroplane'. These extraordinary biplane bombers had a wingspan greater than the iconic Avro Lancaster and B-17 Flying Fortress of the Second World War, while dwarfing any Luftwaffe bomber of that

same period. One 'Giant' was adapted to carry a single 1,000kg bomb, the heaviest type dropped from the air during the war. As the danger posed by these aeroplane attacks increased, ordinary people sought shelter wherever they could find it, and in September 1917 as many as 300,000 Londoners regularly crowded into Underground stations during an intense eight-night period of bombing – a portent of what was yet to come in 1940 and 1941.

By the spring of 1918, the air defences of Britain had come a long way since the early weeks of the war and made giant leaps forward in the previous 12 months. At the time of the first Gotha raid on the capital, the guns defending London and its approaches fired just 360 rounds, but when the last raid took place 11 months later, in May 1918, the L.A.D.A. guns blasted over 30,000 rounds skywards. As they did so, aircraft of the Royal Air Force now hunted the raiders, the RAF newly formed in April 1918 from an amalgamation of the RFC and RNAS.

THE TALLY

German airships dropped about 196 tons of bombs on Britain during the war, causing damage estimated at the time at £1,527,585, killing 557 people and injuring 1,358. Aeroplanes – Gothas, 'Giants' and various seaplanes and landplanes – added another 73 tons, which inflicted further damage estimated at £1,434,526, and killed 857 while injuring 2,058.

This first aerial war over Britain ended without breaking the morale of the people, but it had resulted in traumatic scenes played out across the country as bombs reduced homes to shattered piles of smoking rubble, killing, maiming and mutilating their occupants, from the tiniest baby to the elderly who had been born years before an aeroplane ever flew.

The face of war had changed irrevocably – aerial warfare and the opening of the Home Front, both virtually unheard of before the summer of 1914, were here to stay. It was, though, only the first 'Blitz'. ■

Above Zeppelin L 33 was brought down at Great Wigborough, Essex, on the night of 23/24 September 1916 after raiding London and was set on fire by its crew.
Below Searchlights bracket a Zeppelin over London in October 1915 in a photograph taken for the London Illustrated News.
Right An unexpected reaction to air raids was the market for comic postcards which offered a wry view of the attacks. Huge numbers were sent to family and friends.

Good gracious! you haven't been in a raid, have you?

Oh no! they had some beer at the Red Lion, and I tried to get in!

Beachfront Broadside

German raids against Britain usually involved air attacks, but during the First World War the German Navy also shelled several British towns from the sea.

Although geographically the closest town to Germany, the residents of Lowestoft were not particularly concerned that war would come to them in any real way when it broke out in August 1914. However, on the night of 15/16 April 1915 that complacency was dispelled when the town was raided by a Zeppelin. Terrifying though it was, the attack resulted in relatively little damage although it was a portent of things to come. War would arrive in Lowestoft with a vengeance just over a year later.

Plans to bombard towns on the east coast at daybreak on 25 April 1916, from the cruisers and destroyers of a battlecruiser squadron, along with Zeppelin raids the night before, were intended to entice the Royal Navy to battle. If successful, the High Seas Fleet might destroy significant elements of the British Fleet, reducing or eliminating the Royal Navy's numerical superiority. In

addition, it was timed to coincide with an expected Easter Rebellion by Irish Nationalists.

As targets, Lowestoft and Great Yarmouth were selected because the former was a minelaying and minesweeping base, while Great Yarmouth housed submarines disrupting German movements. The destruction of harbours and military establishments there would assist the war effort - even if it failed to bait the British.

In a well thought out plan, with eight Zeppelins dropping bombs and providing reconnaissance, the ships could assist if an airship was lost over water. Two U-boats were also sent ahead to Lowestoft, while others laid mines against vessels despatched south to engage the German force.

'BOMBS UNLAWFULLY DROPPED'

At noon on the 24th, operations began with the intention of putting the

bombardment group off Lowestoft and Yarmouth by daybreak to bombard them for 30 minutes. But, at 16:00, disaster struck as the battlecruiser *Seydlitz*, in the vanguard of the force, hit a mine and was forced to turn back with a 50 ft gash in her hull.

The British, aware that the German ships had sailed, received information at 20:15 they were heading for Yarmouth and at 15:50 the fleet was put on two-hours-notice, finally ordered south from Scapa Flow at 19:05. Around midnight, the Harwich squadron of three light cruisers and 18 destroyers was ordered north.

Meanwhile, the airships had dropped their bombs while reporting visibility over land as poor, the winds unfavourable and the towns better defended than thought. However, whilst causing widespread terror, the bombs only resulted in one death: 79-year-old Fanny Gaze at Hall Farm, Horning, with the coroner later recording:

Facing Page A German painting by the artist Professor Hans Bohrdt of the bombardment of Lowestoft on 25 April 1916.
Right This imposing house on the Esplanade was cut in two by one of the German naval shells.
Below Left A series of commemorative postcards were produced to mark the bombardment of Lowestoft, this card showing damage at Cleveland Road.
Below Right Bombardment of another of Britain's coastal towns had taken place in Scarborough on 16 December 1915, the devastating assault being used as a tool to encourage enlistment.

LOWESTOFT BOMBARDMENT APRIL 25 1916. PRIVATE HOUSE, ESPLANADE.

'Heart failure from shock endured by the terrifying effect of explosions produced by bombs unlawfully dropped from a Zeppelin aircraft.'

Finally, at 03:50, one of the German ships sighted British ships to the WSW which turned south, attempting to draw the Germans away from Lowestoft. Instead, the four battlecruisers opened fire on the town at 04:10, the terrifying bombardment lasting for ten minutes before the ships moved their attention to Yarmouth. Here, fog made targeting difficult and only a few shells were fired before reports arrived that a British force had engaged the remainder of the German ships, the battlecruisers then breaking off to join them. Yarmouth had had a lucky escape.

Unable to draw the Germans away, the Royal Navy turned towards the Lowestoft attackers, engaging the light cruisers and escorts but broke-off when outgunned by the battlecruisers which had caused severe damage to the cruiser HMS *Conquest* and destroyer HMS *Laertes* and slightly damaged a light cruiser. The Germans then ceased fire, turned NW and hoped in vain that the British cruisers would follow.

During the bombardment, the German light cruiser *Frankfurt* sank one patrol steamer, while the leader of a torpedo-boat flotilla sank another, the crews being rescued and taken POW. However, while battle at sea continued, havoc had been wreaked ashore in Lowestoft.

DEATH, DESTRUCTION & FAILURE
Fortunately, casualties were remarkably light amidst large-scale destruction and only three civilians lost their lives, despite the intensity of the attack: siblings Herbert and Annie Davey and eight-month-old Robert Mumford were killed while Robert's mother, along with Herbert and Annie's parents and their

two other children, were injured when a shell collapsed the upper floor of their home at 20 Sandringham Road. In addition, there was one service death: Petty Officer William Hollis being killed at North End House, the RN Anti-Aircraft HQ on Yarmouth Road.

Light though casualties were, damage was estimated at the then considerable sum of £25,000. Captain Jasper Mayne, East Suffolk's Chief Constable, reported:

'*Damage as follows:- Convalescent Home and Porter's Lodge considerably; Headquarters RNAAS wrecked and gutted by fire; Swimming baths, London Road South, extensively; Claremont Pier land end extensively; South Pier, Naval Base, damaged; 40 dwelling houses extensively; 200 dwelling houses slightly; the telephone wires and tramway wires with part of London Road South near Swimming Bath were demolished, four shells exploded in the enclosure round the wireless station at North Lowestoft...shells were 11-inch and generally made cavities of about 10ft diameter x 3ft deep.*'

The destruction would likely have been worse had the battlecruisers carried high explosive shells rather than

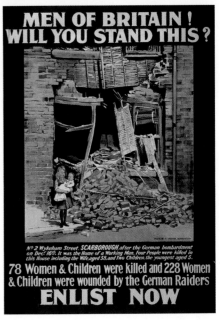

MEN OF BRITAIN!
WILL YOU STAND THIS?

No 2 Wykeham Street, SCARBOROUGH after the German bombardment on Dec 16th. It was the Home of a Working Man. Four People were killed in this House including the Wife, aged 58, and Two Children, the youngest aged 5.
78 Women & Children were killed and 228 Women & Children were wounded by the German Raiders
ENLIST NOW

armour piercing ones. In many cases, these merely created large holes and left unexploded ordnance lying in the streets.

For the Germans, the operation was a dismal failure, sinking only two patrol craft and a submarine by U-boat and damaging one cruiser and a destroyer. Meanwhile, the U-boats found no targets with one sunk and another captured after running-aground at Harwich. The Germans also took serious damage to a battlecruiser, only inflicted light damage to naval establishments at Yarmouth and Lowestoft and failed to take advantage of superior numbers to engage the British.

British casualties were 21 servicemen killed at sea and four persons killed and 19 wounded in Lowestoft. While the raid angered the British, the bombardment of towns and the killing of civilians cost the Germans dearly in world opinion. ∎

3 September 1939
WAR IS DECLARED
War is declared against Germany and air raid sirens sound as a precautionary measure against anticipated air raids.

6 September 1939
BATTLE OF BARKING CREEK
An air attack scare results in confusion and RAF Spitfire and Hurricane fighters do battle with each other in 'friendly fire'. One pilot is killed.

16 October 1939
FIRST AIR RAIDS
The first air attack against the British Isles is launched as German bombers target shipping in the Firth of Forth.

28 October 1939
FIRST ENEMY AIRCRAFT DOWNED
The first enemy aircraft to be brought down on mainland Britain is shot down by Spitfires in the Lammermuir Hills of Scotland.

Blitz Timeline

The Blitz is thought of as the air campaign of 7 September 1940 to 11 May 1941, but this work covers all German air attacks against Britain during the Second World War period.

8 August 1940
CHANNEL CONVOY ATTACKED
Large air attacks against a convoy in the English Channel resulting in the largest air battles of the war to date and sinking of several ships.

10 July 1940
BATTLE OF BRITAIN BEGINS
The date retrospectively set by the British as the commencement of the Battle of Britain, its conclusion considered to be 31 October 1940.

13 November 1939
FIRST BOMBS FALL ON BRITISH SOIL
The first enemy bombs to fall on British soil explode harmlessly in fields at Sullom in the Shetlands.

10 July 1940
BATTLE OF BRITAIN BEGINS
The date retrospectively set by the British as the commencement of the Battle of Britain, its conclusion considered to be 31 October 1940.

7 September 1940
START OF THE BLITZ
Heavy daylight attacks on London continue into the night and herald the commencement of what is generally regarded as The Blitz proper.

21 March 1940
FIRST SHIP SUNK IN ENGLISH CHANNEL
The SS Barn Hill, is bombed off Beachy Head and becomes the first of many ships sunk in the English Channel by German air action.

6 July 1940
DAYLIGHT BOMBING IN BRITAIN
Although not the first date when the Luftwaffe bombed mainland Britain, air attacks took place on Shotton, Plymouth and Aldershot.

1 May 1940
FIRST CIVILIAN DEATHS
A Heinkel 111 crashes and explodes in Clacton-on-Sea killing two civilians who become the first to die as a result of enemy air action.

23 June 1940
AIR OPERATIONS AGAINST BRITAIN START
From the German perspective, this was officially the commencement of Luftwaffe air operations against Britain ('Luftschlact um England')

14 November 1940
BOMBING OF COVENTRY
A huge night attack on Coventry on 14/15 November causes devastation, a large loss of life and the destruction of Coventry Cathedral.

23 November 1940
SOUTHAMPTON BLITZ
Southampton came under air attack earlier in 1940, but a major attack on the night of 23/24 November esulted in significant destruction.

12 & 15 December 1940
THE SHEFFIELD BLITZ
An important steel and armaments city, Sheffield comes under sustained attack and suffers considerable damage and heavy casualties.

20 & 22 December 1940
LIVERPOOL'S 'CHRISTMAS BLITZ'
As an important port, Liverpool was high on the list of targets and came under sustained assault at the end of December with over 300 casualties.

22 & 23 December 1940
MANCHESTER'S 'CHRISTMAS BLITZ'
One of Britain's big cities which came in for attention was Manchester which also suffered heavily in pre-Christmas attacks.

2 January 1941
THE CARDIFF BLITZ
On 2 January 1941 the Luftwaffe turned its attention on Cardiff with the cathedral being badly damaged by a Luftmine which fell nearby.

19 February 1941
THE SWANSEA BLITZ
Gradually, the Luftwaffe was working its way around all of the major cities in the British Isles, with Swansea coming under heavy attack.

13 & 14 March 1941
CLYDEBANK BLITZ
On the night of 13 March 1941, it was the turn of Clydebank to come under assault as 236 bombers laid waste to large swathes of the area.

3 March 1943
BETHNAL GREEN TUBE STATION DISASTER
Heavy loss of life when civilians rushing to get into the station were caught in a crush on the stairs. 173 people died and many were injured.

27 April 1942
BAEDECKER RAID ON NORWICH
As a continuation of the Baedecker raids, the city of Norwich comes under heavy attack.

23 April 1942
BAEDECKER RAID ON EXETER
The Luftwaffe carried out an attack in the so-called Baedecker Raids, supposedly based around a German tourist guide of Britain.

4 March 1942
TIP AND RUN ATTACKS COMMENCE
Luftwaffe high command authorises formation of units to commence fighter-bomber attacks on Southern England known as Tip and Run attacks.

11 May 1941
LONDON'S LAST BIG RAIDS OF THE BLITZ
On the night of 10/11 May 1941 the last major attack of The Blitz was carried out on London which killed 1,436 people and injured 1,792.

1 May 1941
LIVERPOOL'S MAY BLITZ
After the attacks just before Christmas, the bombers returned to Merseyside in a series of big raids with 681 bombers attacking the city.

15 April 1941
THE BELFAST BLITZ
Over Easter Belfast came in for a pounding, the British traitor known as 'Lord Haw-Haw' spoke mockingly of 'Easter Eggs for Belfast'.

20 & 21 March 1941
PLYMOUTH'S MARCH RAIDS
As a Royal Navy dockyard, Plymouth was an obvious target and came under heavy overnight attack in raids which began at around 8.39

21 January 1944
OPERATION STEINBOCK COMMENCESThe Luftwaffe commenced air raids against London in response to the Allied air attacks on Germany. The operation was a tactical failure.

12 June 1944
FIRST V1 BOMBS LAUNCHED ON ENGLAND
On the night of 12/13 June 1944, the first of what would be 9,251 Flying bombs was launched against London in the V1 campaign.

8 September 1944
FIRST V2 ROCKET LAUNCHED on BRITAIN
A new phase in the air assault on Britain commenced and lasted until March 1945. The V2s killed 2,754 and seriously injured 6,523.

3/4 March 1945
LAST AIRCRAFT DOWNED IN BRITAIN
On this night, three Junkers 88 aircraft crashed in Yorkshire, Suffolk and Lincolnshire and became the last enemy aircraft downed on British soil.

27 March 1945
LAST CIVILIAN CASUALTY
The last V2 rocket to fall in Britain fell on this day and resulted in the last civilian death in Britain due to enemy action.

29 March 1945
LAST V1 FLYING BOMB FALLS
The final V1 Flying Bomb to come down in Britain falls at Datchworth, Hertforshire.

The First of Many

During the Second World War, around 1,200 enemy aircraft were brought down over the British Isles, the first coming down on the mainland of the British Isles in Scotland, just weeks after the outbreak of war.

At 09.15 hrs on Saturday 28 October 1939, three Spitfires of Red Section, 603 Squadron, got airborne from RAF Turnhouse for a routine patrol at 14,000 ft over the River Forth whilst at the same time, three Spitfires of Red Section, 602 Squadron, were already patrolling overhead. Already, in little over one month of war, raiders regularly operated against targets around Scotland and the north of England, with 602 and 603 Squadrons claiming victories over the North Sea against Junkers 88s and a Heinkel 111 on 16 and 22 October.

Operating at long range over the North Sea, the raids were risky for the Luftwaffe. Conducted during daylight, and with no fighter cover, the raiders were flying into sensitive and well-defended areas: the strategically important Scapa Flow and the shipyards and docks of the Clyde off to the west. The region was patrolled constantly by the squadrons of RAF Fighter Command's 13 Group, and it was into this 'hot' area that Leutnant Rolf Niehoff brought his Stab./KG26 crew that morning, as captain of Heinkel 111, Werk Nummer 5449, 1H+JA. His mission was

armed reconnaissance. First, to Glasgow, then back eastwards to look out for British ships in the Firth of Forth.

As the first Luftwaffe aircraft over the British Isles that morning, Niehoff was under orders to transmit a weather report once he reached the coast. Later, he concluded the wireless transmission had been his undoing, having been heard by the British and alerting them to his presence. However, that was not the case.

Returning from the west coast at 15,000 ft, Niehoff discovered the earlier cloud cover had thinned over the Forth, giving

The War Illustrated,' Week Ending November 18th, 1939   *Registered at the G.P.O. as a Newspaper*

Vol. 1 FIRST & ONLY PHOTO-RECORD OF THE SECOND GREAT WAR No. 10

THE WAR ILLUSTRATED

3d Weekly

Edited by
SIR JOHN
HAMMERTON
Editor of "THE WAR ILLUSTRATED" (1914-1920)
"WORLD WAR, 1914-1918," "I WAS THERE!" etc.

First Enemy 'Plane Down in Britain ★ ★ ★ ★ ★ ★ EXCLUSIVE HISTORIC PHOTOS IN THIS NUMBER

FIRST BOMBS

Although the first air attack on targets within the British Isles was the raid conducted against naval shipping in the Firth of Forth on 16 October 1939, the first German bombs of the Second World War to explode on British soil fell at Sullom in the Shetlands at 13.00 hours on Monday 13 November 1939.

In this incident, four bombs fell harmlessly on farmland, with the British news media seeing an opportunity to pronounce how risibly ineffective German bombs were. To illustrate the un-threatening nature of Luftwaffe attacks, the newspaper photographer pictured a local man, John Halcrow, standing in one of the bomb craters holding a dead rabbit - supposedly the only casualty.

In fact, the 'casualty' was a rabbit purchased from a local butcher and simply used for photographic effect to illustrate that all the Germans could achieve for their effort was to kill rabbits! On the other hand, when the photograph emerged in Germany, the propaganda machine there put their own rather different spin on things and published the same photograph on 25 November 1939 with the following caption:

There Is No Treatment For Intellectual Poverty, Mr. Churchill

At last, Winston Churchill has a new idea! He put a man into the crater left by a German aerial bomb on the Shetland islands. In one hand the brave Englishman had to hold a rabbit, the 'only' victim of a German bombing raid, and in the other a bomb splinter. With such inanities they are unable to disparage the achievements of the German aviator, nor will it be possible to reverse concern about the constant achievements of the Luftwaffe which is present among the English people.

Above John Halcrow poses in one of the bomb craters on the Shetlands, holding a bomb splinter and a rabbit which was supposedly killed by the bomb.

a much better opportunity to photograph shipping. Unfortunately, the thinning cloud was a two-edged sword; it also gave anti-aircraft gunners a better view of the roaming Heinkel III and immediately the gunners put up a barrage from shipping at anchor off Queensferry, including HMS *Belfast*, HMS *Edinburgh* and HMS *Mohawk*.

Rolf Niehoff takes up the story:

"When we returned from Glasgow, we were greeted by anti-aircraft fire. One shot must have been a hit because I heard the explosion and felt the impact, but I do not think much damage was done."

However, while the damage was not critical, it still sealed his fate and the Spitfires of 602 and 603 Squadrons were alerted by the bursting shells and were quickly in hot pursuit of the bomber.

Again, we turn to Niehoff's account:

"A short time after the anti-aircraft fire, four Spitfires appeared and began

Left The first enemy aircraft brought down on British soil across what would turn out be just over five years of almost relentless air attacks was this Heinkel 111 H-2 of Stab./KG26, shot down at Long Newton Farm, Humbie, Scotland, on 28 October 1939.
Right The shooting down of the Heinkel 111 at Humbie attracted the attention of news outlets, with the arrival on British soil of an enemy aircraft then considered a novelty. This was the front cover of 'The War Illustrated' from 18 November 1939.

attacking - one after the other. My two rear gunners were at their weapons and alert. They were Gefreiter Bruno Reimann and Unteroffizier Gottlieb Kowalke. Twice before, we'd had contact with enemy fighters but this time my gunners started shooting far too early, so that the first Spitfire killed them both as they were changing spent ammunition drums.

Top A Luftwaffe crew member of KG26 counts the bullet holes in a Heinkel 111 which managed to get home.
Above Flight Lieutenant 'Pat' Gifford of 603 Squadron photographed after an action during the raid of 16 October 1939 when he was involved in shooting down a Junkers 88 over the Firth of Forth.

Before I could go to look after my gunners, my young but very able pilot, Unteroffizier Kurt Lehmkuhl, was hit in the back by two bullets and I had to stay with him in the cockpit in case he fainted.

Now, the Spitfires got no more fire from our aircraft and flew close to our rear. Therefore, most of their bullets hit our wings and engines which soon stopped. Only a few more bullets hit the cockpit, which is why I and my pilot survived. The four Spitfires were shooting at us until we hit the ground."

Meanwhile, Yellow Section of 602 Squadron were ordered off to find and engage the enemy, but the Spitfires instead found an RAF Anson off May Island. Flt Lt Hodge, mistaking the Anson for an enemy aircraft, led his section in for an attack and raked the RAF aircraft with gunfire before the error was realised, but not before the Anson pilot was hit and wounded in the jaw.

The attacking pilots of 603 Squadron who engaged the Heinkel were Flt Lt P Gifford, Plt Off C Robertson and Plt Off G K Gilroy, and although Red Section of 602 Squadron reportedly engaged the Heinkel first, only Flt Lt A A 'Archie' McKellar actually did so with any success. However, far from Niehoff's air gunners opening fire too early, McKellar reported one Spitfire got a bullet through a wing spar and ammunition pan. With 602 Squadron's Spitfires first into attack, they had been fired on before the Heinkel's defensive fire was silenced.

Wounded in the back, weak from loss of blood and still under attack by four Spitfires which were now queuing up to pump more lead into his aircraft, Kurt Lehmkuhl did a creditable job of getting the Heinkel down to a reasonable crash-landing in less-than-ideal terrain. With insufficient height to bale-out and two dead engines, he had no choice.

In what was a rapid descent over the Lammermuir Hills, Lehmkuhl had selected the only place available to land which was a heather covered slope directly ahead of him. The spot he had selected was between High Latch and Kidlaw, east of Humbie village, the bomber becoming the first enemy aircraft down intact on mainland British soil during the war.

THE KG26 EMBLEM

The emblem of Kampfgeschwader 26 with its motto 'Vestigium Leonis', which might loosely be translated as 'In the Lion's Footsteps'. Different elements of KG26 wore this emblem on their aircraft with various coloured shields. The Humbie aircraft had a white shield.

Above Right A Heinkel 111 of KG26 is prepared for another sortie.
Right The Luftwaffe target map for the Forth Bridge, the same area seen in the photographs of the 16 October 1939 raid.

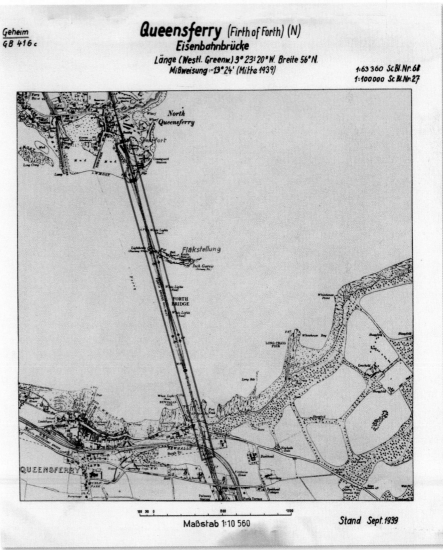

Careering over rough terrain and demolishing a stone wall where it left its starboard tailplane, the bullet-riddled Heinkel came to rest uphill, its nose smashed and its back broken. But it was not only the Heinkel with a broken back.

The bumpy landing had literally been bone-jarring, and Rolf Niehoff, unhurt in the fighter assault, was later found to have a broken back, caused as the Heinkel juddered to a halt.

However, his injuries did not prevent him from getting his wounded pilot out of the aircraft. Reimann and Gottleib were beyond help, but Niehoff tended to his wounded pilot before the first people arrived at the crash site.

The landing caused great excitement for local civilians, and such was the novelty of Luftwaffe aircraft landing in Britain at that time that the BBC broadcast an interview with local farmer John Irvine:

'I was filling up sacks of barley about a quarter past ten when I heard a noise like the hurling of a barrow. That's what I thought it was at first, but it went on and on and came nearer, and then I knew it was the noise of guns. Then we saw a big black machine with two engines coming over the trees from the north-west. There were four British machines with it. They were circling round and round and rattling bullets into the German.

I thought we ought to take cover, there were women workers there, but curiosity brought us out again. The whiles we were running in, and the whiles we were running out again, so that we saw the German go over the houses, so low it almost touched the chimneys. Then they all went out of sight up over the hill, and a few minutes later I saw our fighters going back, all four of them. They seemed to be finished with the job, so I ran up to see what had happened.

Two of the crew were dead. They must be the gunners and must have been shot

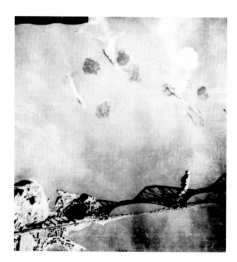

Above The attack on Royal Navy ships in the Firth of Forth on 16 October 1940, with the shadow of the famous rail bridge clearly visible. During this attack, the captain of the aircraft brought down at Humbie on 28 October 1939 took photographs of the raid. This is possibly one of those photographs and shows bomb bursts in the water around the ships.

Right The Luftwaffe photo for the Forth Bridge, the same area seen in the photographs of the 16 October 1939 raid.

before they came my length, because I never saw them firing at our 'planes. The machine scraped its tail over a dyke and came down on the moor on an even keel. One of the crew was not hurt at all. He was pulling out his mate. By the time we got up there he had him out and on the ground.

We tried to talk to the unwounded man, but he did not know what we were saying, although he spoke a little English. The wounded man said he wanted a drink, but the doctor said he ought not have one. He had two bullet wounds in the back.

The Police took the unwounded man away, and before he went, he shook hands with his mate. We got a gate and carried the wounded man down to the road and waited for the ambulance to come for him.'

Albeit John Irvine thought one man (Niehoff) was unwounded, that was not so, a contemporary photograph showing Rolf Niehoff with Police officers and holds a hand to his hurt back.

Niehoff takes up the story:

"A few minutes after the crash, some men arrived and among them a Doctor who took care of my wounded pilot. He was later taken to an Edinburgh hospital.

"I was taken prisoner by some friendly policemen and to a police station in Dalkeith. I waited until an Army Captain arrived and took me in his private car to the HQ of an army unit in a country estate. Here, a Colonel received me and asked me my name and home address, but then added: 'I don't suppose you will answer any other questions?' Of course, I wouldn't! Then, he took me to the mess where I chatted with the officers there before the Captain invited me to lunch in his room. Afterwards, I was taken to Edinburgh Castle and spent the afternoon in the guard room.

During that afternoon I was interviewed by two RAF officers. They asked me which of the four Spitfires shot me down, but I didn't know.

That night, I was taken to London by train, guarded by four armed soldiers. After arrival, I was taken straight to the Tower of London where the treatment was very correct but strictly military. It was not always so with the following interrogation.

In the Tower, I shared a room with Oberleutnant Heinrich Storp who was shot down over the Firth of Forth on 16 October in a Junkers 88 that crashed into the sea. Strangely, I had been on that same raid! During the raid, I took photos of the HMS Edinburgh and HMS Southampton. To my surprise, I later saw these photographs in the magazine 'Picture Post'.

"After some days in the Tower, I was taken for X-Rays at Westminster Hospital, and then to the Royal Herbert Military Hospital, Woolwich, to be treated for a broken back."

In the early days of the war, the British had not established arrangements for housing prisoners during their first days of captivity, the Tower of London being used initially for this purpose - something Niehoff regarded as a badge of honour:

"After all, the Tower of London was traditionally used to imprison enemies of the British Monarch. And I was most definitely an 'enemy' of The King!" ■

Roof over Britain

An ever-present feature of the air war over Britain was anti-aircraft fire, with batteries of guns spread the length and breadth of Britain. Anti-aircraft defences during the Blitz, though, were often more dangerous to friend than they were to foe.

The failure of the campaign in Norway convinced General Sir Frederick Pile, C-in-C of Anti-Aircraft Command, of the paramount need for anti-aircraft defences, and thus pressed for and secured a large expansion of the Command and its weaponry during 1940.

At the outbreak of war, the total number of heavy anti-aircraft guns in the Command stood at 695, many of which were of old and obsolescent. The approved and recommended total at this time stood at 2,232 guns, and the position with light anti-aircraft guns was

worse, with there being only 253 out of an approved total of 1,200. Of the best light anti-aircraft gun, the 40mm Bofors, there were only 76.

The increase in equipment levels, after General Pile's pressuring for adequate resources, was still way below minimum requirements by the time of the Blitz. However, at the end of 1939, there were only 850 heavy guns, 510 light guns and 3,361 searchlights. At the beginning of July 1940, there were 1,200 Heavy guns, 549 Light guns and 3,932 Searchlights, with the position continuing to improve after the Blitz began.

By May 1941, when the Blitz proper ended, 1,691 heavy Guns, 940 light guns and 4,532 searchlights were operational.

As for manpower, and the result of the introduction of conscription in 1939, it was intended to allot 20,000 troops every three months to help man these defences. By July 1940, the total manpower in Anti-Aircraft Command stood at 157,319.

Whilst the effectiveness of anti-aircraft guns is debatable, they were a significant part of Britain's air defence system. The numbers of enemy aircraft destroyed or damaged by anti-aircraft guns was

Born in 1884, Frederick Alfred Pile (2nd Baronet) was commissioned into the Royal Artillery in 1904, serving in India before the First World War. In 1914, he was involved in the retreat from Mons as a Staff Captain with the 1st Division. He became a Brigade Major with 40th Division in 1916, and in the closing stages of the war became a General Staff Officer with 22nd Corps in France. After the war, he was appointed Brigade Major with the Brighton and Shoreham District, before transfer to the Royal Tank Corps in 1923.
In 1928, he became Commander of the 1st Experimental Mechanised Force, and then Assistant Director of Mechanisation at the War Office. He went to Egypt in 1932, as Commander of the Canal Brigade (Mechanised Force) before becoming General Officer Commanding 1st Anti-Aircraft Division in 1937 and, in 1939, being made General Officer Commanding-in-Chief of Anti-Aircraft Command. This was a position he held until 1945.
He became the only British General to retain his same command throughout the entire war. He died in 1976.

Above General Sir Frederick Pile, Bt., D.S.O., M.C., General Officer Commanding-in-Chief, Anti-Aircraft Command, 1939-45.

Left The 4.5-inch anti-aircraft gun battery at Mudchute, on London's Isle of Dogs. The installation was initially manned by the 154 Battery of the 52nd (London) Heavy Anti-Aircraft Regiment, Territorial Army. **Above** A 3.7-inch gun battery in action during the London Blitz. The sound of the guns firing, and the shells exploding high above, gave a feeling of some security to many on the ground. In many respects, it turned out to be a misplaced feeling.

proportionately low given the scale of effort employed and number of rounds fired. However, it is difficult to assess the actual effect that anti-aircraft fire had on German bomber formations although it undoubtedly played a part in disrupting such attacks, often greatly affecting the morale of bomber crews.

A DEADLY RAIN

On the other hand, though, gunfire could be equally dangerous to friend as well as to foe during the Blitz. And, arguably, quite likely more dangerous to the former rather than the latter!

As the saying goes: 'Whatever goes up must come down'. And so it was with anti-aircraft fire: falling shell splinters and unexploded shells fell back to earth. This frequently resulted in damage, death, or injury. Not only that, but many shells had defective timing mechanisms meaning that instead of exploding at 12,000 feet, they plunged to earth and exploded on impact.

In fact, it was estimated that half the shells fired exploded at ground level and, astonishingly, killed as many people as

did German bombs. If true, then anti-aircraft artillery was responsible for over 25,000 deaths in Britain during the Second World War.

On Sunday, 8 September 1940 - the day after the Blitz began – an anti-aircraft artillery shell landed outside a café near Kings Cross, killing 17 people. From then on, the death toll on the ground from anti-aircraft fire was constant and unrelenting. And neither were such deaths limited to London. It would be a deadly rain.

On 14 September 1940, members of the Women's Royal Naval Service (WRENS) were sitting down to dinner in Lee-on-Solent where they were billeted. A shell fired in Portsmouth smashed through the window of their dining room and exploded, killing 10 of the young women outright.

In some areas, though, there is no question but that more people were killed by anti-aircraft shells than by bombs. In the Midlands district of Tipton, 23 civilians are recording as having been killed during air raids.

Of these, 11 deaths were caused by German bombs, but the other 12 died during an incident on 21 December 1940, when a wedding party was taking place in a pub in the village of Tividale. Here, a shell crashed down the chimney of the building where the party was being held. The bride was killed, the bridegroom lost both legs and 11 other guests died.

However, the number of injuries and deaths from anti-aircraft fire was not entirely unknown in the wider civilian population. Sometimes, it was even

reported in both national and provincial newspapers, despite censorship. On 29 March 1944, for example, the Western Mail reported that:

'Anti-aircraft shells, one of which exploded in a crowded factory, killing 12 people, including seven women, and injuring as many more, were the chief cause of damage during activity over the South Wales coastal area on Monday night.'

Nevertheless, the Ministry of Information sought to reassure the public and, in 1942, produced a booklet called 'Roof Over Britain', extolling the value

Right The Gun Operations Room (GOR) for the 1st Ant-Aircraft Division in London's Brompton Road tube station.
Below Left The Anti-Aircraft Command shoulder patch which can be seen worn on the upper sleeves of the women plotters in the Gun Operations Room.
Below Right The suitably heroic cover of the 1942 booklet, 'Roof over Britain', with artwork by war artist Abram Games.
Bottom Right Dangerous 'rain': this anti-aircraft splinter is typical of those which rained down during air raids when the guns were firing. Many thought they were fragments of bombs, and the finder of this wartime souvenir had mistakenly labelled it: 'German bomb shrapnel.'

of anti-aircraft defences. For his part, General Sir Frederick Pile put a 'spin' on things:

'The volume of fire which resulted, and which was publicised as a 'barrage', was in fact largely wild and uncontrolled shooting. There were, however, two valuable results from it: the volume of fire had a deterrent effect upon at least some of the aircrews and there was a marked improvement in civilian morale.'

Had they been fully aware of the danger posed, then maybe the civilian population would have been less enthused about things.

Putting things into perspective, during September 1940, for example, anti-aircraft gunners defending London fired a quarter of a million shells at night, mostly into thin air. Their efforts accounted for well under a dozen enemy aircraft; just one aircraft for every 30,000 shells fired.

In addition, the numbers of enemy aircraft claimed as destroyed was a vast over-estimate, it being stated that one enemy aircraft was destroyed by anti-aircraft fire to every two by fighters, the total claim for the first two years of the war being 600 destroyed. The figure is hugely less than that, and only in

relatively low double figures.

Despite the relative paucity of anti-aircraft success, they did give some measure of 'comfort' to the British public who at least felt they were .being defended as the guns barked defiantly.

The 'Roof over Britain', however, tended to be far more dangerous to friend than it was to foe. And the 'rain' it allowed in could be lethal. ■

DEADLY DANGER

If anti-aircraft shells exploded at altitude as intended, then the shell splinters rained earthwards in deadly cascades of red-hot jagged steel shards. Being hit by one of these fragments could cause serious injury, or worse.

Also falling earthwards from the shell bursts were the fuse caps from the nose of the shells. Again, these could cause serious damage to property and, potentially, result in serious or life-threatening injuries. Very often, shells did not explode as

intended and fell back to earth. On these occasions, the projectile often detonated on impact. With such explosions happening during the height of an air raid, so the resulting detonation would often be taken for a bomb. The result was that very many people were killed or injured by 'friendly' anti-aircraft shells. Often, it would simply not be realised what the cause of the blast had been. And for those shells which did not explode, so Bomb Disposal teams were kept almost as busy dealing with these as they were German UXBs.

Defence Equipment

A whole range of guns, weaponry and other defensive measures were employed throughout the Second World War to defend Britain against aerial attack from both aircraft and the V1 Flying Bomb menace. These defences ranged from heavy artillery pieces to light ant-aircraft weapons, rocket launchers, searchlights and sound locators.

QF 3-INCH 20-CWT

The 3-inch Heavy Anti-aircraft (HAA) gun was originally adopted during the First World War, where it became the principal and most effective AA gun then in service. It fired a shell of 16 pounds with a muzzle velocity of 2,000 feet per second. Its effective range was 16,000 ft with maximum ceiling of 22,000 ft.

When the British Expeditionary Force deployed to France in 1939, 48 x 3-inch guns were sent with them. It had been suggested that the BEF should be equipped with the newer 3.7-inch HAA gun, but those responsible for making such decisions in the BEF stated they preferred to keep the 3-inch guns. So, by chance, many of the HAA guns left in France after Dunkirk were the older 3-inch 20-cwt guns rather than the modern 3-7-inch HAA guns that would be needed in the air defence of Great Britain during the Blitz.

A few of the surviving 3 Inch guns remained in use, briefly, for home defence in 1940.

Above The QF 3-inch heavy anti-aircraft gun. A few of these obsolete guns remained in service in 1940. Many of them, like these, were left behind at Dunkirk after the withdrawal from France.

Z BATTERY

The Z Battery was a short range anti-aircraft weapon system, which launched 3-inch diameter rockets from ground-based single and multiple launchers.

In October 1940, an experimental Z Battery became operational at Cardiff, South Wales, under the command of Major Duncan Sandys, Prime Minister Winston Churchill's son-in-law.

The first Z Batteries were equipped with single-rocket launchers, the Projector, 3-inch, Mark 1, but it was found the rockets did not perform as accurately as trials had suggested and that the proximity fuses were rarely effective. Therefore, the technique of firing rockets in large salvos was introduced, and projectors capable of firing ever-larger numbers of rockets were developed.

From early 1942, the manning of Z Batteries was transferred to the Home Guard*, as the equipment was comparatively simple to operate and the rounds were lighter than for conventional guns. However, the success of these devices was extremely poor.

*Note: On 3 March 1943, civilians queueing to enter Bethnal Green Underground station in East London, which was being used at night as an air raid shelter, were panicked by the noise of a newly installed Z Battery firing in nearby Victoria Park. After somebody tripped on the stairs leading down to the ticket office, some 300 people were crushed in the stairwell. 173 were killed and 90 needed hospital treatment. Indirectly, yet more casualties caused by anti-aircraft weaponry.

Above The Z-Battery rocket projector.

4.5-INCH HEAVY ANTI-AIRCRAFT GUN

At a corresponding time with the development of the 3.7-inch HAA gun, came recognition that an even more powerful high-angle heavy anti-aircraft gun for land service was also required. The gun chosen to fulfil the role was designated as a 4.5-inch gun. Emplaced in static positions, mounted on holdfasts set in concrete, the guns were mounted behind large steel gun shields giving the resemblance of a ship's gun turret. The weight of the gun was 16.5 tons, and it could traverse through 360° and elevate up to 80°. A 55-pound high explosive shell was fired at a muzzle velocity of 2,470 feet per second. The maximum ceiling attainable was 42,000 ft, but its normal operating ceiling was between 22-28,000 ft. The 4.5-inch fired a round weighing 86 pounds and the rate of fire was eight rounds per minute. The first 4.5-inch guns were in place and ready for operation by February 1939.

Above The size of the 4.5-inch HAA shell is demonstrated by these two Royal Navy gunners on HMS Wallace who shot down a Junkers 88 during the late afternoon of 26 January 1941 off Brightlingsea, Essex. The rating on the left holds part of the bomber they had destroyed.
Right A 4.5-inch gun battery stands ready for action during late 1940.

40MM BOFORS GUN

One of the best-known light anti-aircraft guns, the 40mm Bofors gun was an effective weapon in countering the threat of dive-bombers and low flying aircraft but could also be effective against ground targets.

The Bofors fired a 2-pound (40mm) high explosive shell fitted with an impact fuze. The 40mm shell had a muzzle velocity of 2.790 feet per second and could be fired in either single shot or bursts at a rate of 120 rounds per minute.

It was fired by a pedal operated by the loader who fed clips of rounds into an autoloader located on the top of the gun. The Bofors proved to be versatile, reliable, and robust and was responsible for shooting down several low flying enemy aircraft during service with Anti-Aircraft Command.

Above The Bofors 40 mm light anti-aircraft gun.
Right The Bofors handbook illustration for the 40mm shell.

THE VICKERS 2PDR

Classified as a Light Anti-Aircraft (LAA) gun, the Vickers 2pdr (often referred to as the 'Pom Pom') was accepted for land service as an anti-aircraft gun in 1936.

It had a low muzzle velocity (2,300 feet per second), lacked a satisfactory explosive shell and was not provided with tracer ammunition. This is important in a LAA gun to allow the flight of the projectile to be observed, thus allowing fire to be corrected to hit the target. Employed as a stopgap design only, the 2-pdr filled the role of LAA gun until the more suitable 40mm Bofors gun was adopted, although a number were still in service during 1940.

Above The Vickers 2pdr 'Pom-Pom' gun. A small number of these remained in service during 1940.

SOUND DETECTORS

Although sound-ranging was being superseded at the time of the Blitz, it remained in use to a limited extent. As with searchlights, sound-ranging units were part of Anti-Aircraft Command.

Sound ranging was used to determine the distance between a given point and the position of a sound source by measuring the time lapse between the origin of the sound and its arrival at the listening location.

Its use was developed during the First World War, on land, to locate enemy artillery batteries and for air defence to counter the threat of German heavy bombers. Between the wars, sound ranging was developed as a method of locating enemy aircraft.

Sound ranging equipment was utilised for directing searchlight beams and plotting night raids. When working in pairs, they could select where to aim heavy anti-aircraft concentrations. As a technology, sound ranging was outmoded by 1940 and eventually superseded by radar. However, this basic audible system played its part in the early stages of the Blitz.

Right One of the relatively primitive sound locators which was still in use during the early stages of the Blitz.

3.7-INCH GUN

The need for a high performance, purpose designed heavy anti-aircraft gun to replace the 3-inch 20-cwt gun was identified during the 1920's.

Vickers began production of the gun in 1937, but with the gathering storm clouds of war the pace gathered of re-armament in Great Britain and an increased production for this gun was soon recognised as essential. To meet demand, a simpler, static design was introduced where the running gear, legs and raising equipment were eliminated and the gun simply placed on a static mounting which could be bolted on to hold fasts.

The requirement issued was for a gun with a muzzle velocity of 3,000 feet per second, firing a shell with a weight of 28 pounds, with an effective ceiling of 35,000 feet, to be road transportable and weighing no more than eight tons.

This weapon became one of the mainstays of Britain's anti-aircraft defence during the Blitz.

Right A 3.7-inch gun in its emplacement. This photograph, late in the war, shows a gun crew with trophies collected from a German aircraft they had succeeded in destroying. By this stage of the war, ATS women were frequently part of the gun crew complement.

SEARCHLIGHTS

Searchlights were an essential part of night-time defences, a modernisation programme for equipment instituted in 1935. Up to that time, the main equipment was the 120cm* SL Projector, the units equipped with First World War vintage lorries.

The replacement searchlight was the 90cm projector, which was lighter, smaller, and powered by a high-density arc lamp. The beam could be manually directed using visual observation or directed with sound ranging equipment. The searchlight was mounted onto a small, tracked chassis and could be easily transported. To power them, lorry mounted generators were employed.

Just prior to the war, a new 150cm searchlight was introduced. Mounted on a trailer, it produced an intensely bright narrow beam from a high-density carbon arc lamp using a large reflector. It was capable of penetrating mist and low cloud and could illuminate targets up to 20,000 feet.

*Note: Searchlights were designated in centimetres as opposed to inches due to the reflector being an optical instrument. With optical instruments often sourced from Europe, all were measured in cm and mm.

Left The standard 120cm SL projector in use during the Blitz.

Above As with the barrage balloons, women were employed on anti-aircraft gun sites as spotters, range finders and drivers. This ATS girl is a spotter at a 3.7-inch battery in December 1942.

Left By the time of the V1 Flying Bomb campaign in 1944, the anti-aircraft gun had rather more come into its own with a far greater degree of accuracy possible due to radar control. As a result, a considerable number of the weapons were brought down by gun barrages. This remarkable painting by Wilfred Haines shows a V1 'coned' by searchlights over London as it is engaged by the guns. However, this painting has a tragic story attached to it as the artist was subsequently killed in a later V1 Flying Bomb incident. The damage visible on the left of the painting, adjacent to the searchlight beam, was caused in the V1 explosion which killed Wilfred Haines.

The Balloon Barrage

The skyscape of Britain during the Second World War was peppered by silver barrage balloons, tethered on steel cables. The image was one that became synonymous with the Home Front, the balloons as deadly a menace to friendly aircraft as to the enemy.

Balloon barrages, an almost iconic element of wartime Britain, became an integral part of the country's air defence system and although not a particularly 'glamorous' aspect of the air war, balloons were a passive form of defence which proved extremely effective in forcing enemy raiders to fly higher. Thus, given the limited technology of the time, enemy aircraft bombed less accurately. That they were also lethal to our own aircraft, though, was an unfortunate by-product.

Before the war, a separate Balloon Command under the control of RAF Fighter Command was formed, and eventually became responsible for many thousands of balloons covering strategic targets all over Britain. However, the barrage balloon story began towards the end of the First World War, during the first 'Blitz'.

Then, three 'balloon aprons' were employed in the defence of London and were formed by tethering four or five balloons in a single line and stretching a network of light steel cables between them. The weight of these, even using the lightest possible cables, was a serious load on the small buoyancy of the balloons employed for this purpose. The network, too, tended to sag and drew the balloons together into bunches, it then being difficult to lower the entire arrangement without fouling houses, trees and overhead lines.

The Balloon Apron Squadrons were formed with a HQ at Barking, at Woodford in Essex, and at Shooter's Hill in south-east London. Despite problems with handling these balloons, they were considered 'effective' although not so much as a means of destroying enemy aircraft but simply because they forced them to fly at predictable heights which could then be saturated with anti-aircraft fire. At least one Gotha bomber is known to have flown into the cables, but somewhat remarkably it escaped with only slight damage.

Facing Page A barrage balloon being handled by its crew near Biggin Hill, Kent, during the summer of 1944 at the height of the V 1 Flying Bomb campaign. A mass of other balloons can also been seen airborne in the background.

Right This Heinkel 111 of 4./KG 27, fitted with a barrage balloon fender, crashed near Durdle Door, Dorset, during the early evening of 22 May 1941 while on an armed shipping reconnaissance in the English Channel after flying into a mist covered hill. Bizarrely, two of crew were killed after they jumped from the aircraft while it was still moving.

Below Right By the summer of 1940, barrage balloons were a feature of the landscape as well as the skyscape. In this original colour photograph, one balloon is tethered in a London park and another can be seen flying in the distance.

A FORMIDABLE RISK

Since the First World War, much practical experience in the development of balloon barrages had been gained. Within a new Balloon Command coming into being on 1 November 1938, under the command of Air Vice-Marshal O T Boyd, CB, OBE, the Auxiliary Air Force formed Balloon Squadrons which, by August 1940, reached a total of 49.

The renewed requirement for air defences in the 1930s, though, produced an alternative to the apron method. The modern balloon barrage would comprise merely of cables by which the balloons were held captive. Later, extra hanging cables were added, some with explosive devices attached. Unfortunately, by September 1939, balloon production was unable to keep pace with demand so that, on the first day of war, less than half the planned establishment could be deployed: 444 balloons in London and 180 elsewhere in the country.

At first sight, such defences might appear illusory. However, if a few simple calculations are made it can be seen to be more effective than imagined. Assuming an aircraft of 70-foot wingspan passes through a line of balloons tethered at 100-yard intervals there is around one chance in four of hitting a cable - a formidable risk no attacker could afford to take. Even though contemporary bombers of the period were able to reach altitudes above 20,000ft, a balloon barrage, if of sufficient density, might reduce the defending fighters' task of finding the bombers by forcing them higher, with lower altitudes being the murkiest part of the atmosphere and which would otherwise have needed searching.

At that time, low-flying aircraft were the least vulnerable to AA fire and defending fighters. This was because there was insufficient time for guns or searchlight to be trained on the aircraft before it disappeared. Also, intercepting fighters found a raider difficult to spot against backgrounds of countryside or urban sprawl. Thus, balloons served to drive attackers to altitudes where they could be more easily engaged.

Obviously, balloons flown at any altitude in daylight themselves made good targets in fine weather, but such conditions were also those when guns and fighters could operate most effectively. Nigh-time and bad visibility were when balloon barrages were most needed and when they would be immune from attack.

BALLOON VICTIMS AND 'ILL WINDS'

One method of siting balloons was to moor them on the perimeter of the defended area. If sited equidistantly over a circular area, then the probability of impact was two to three times greater, but the effectiveness of barrages might be reduced by flying through them in line-ahead formation with specially equipped aircraft in the lead. However, such a theoretical tactic was nigh-on impossible during darkness. Several Luftwaffe aircraft, though, which operated over Britain were known to be fitted with cable fenders or cutters. At least one Heinkel III brought down was fitted with such a device.

On land, balloons were often flown from winch-equipped lorries for ease of mobility, while permanent sites used combinations of screw pickets, buried railway sleepers and sandbags to hold them down. Initially, the balloons were operated by RAF airmen although as more women were recruited into the WAAF, so it was that a good many WAAFs were posted to balloon squadrons. Sadly, however, their balloon victims would prove to be both friend and foe alike.

One of the first Luftwaffe aircraft to fall to a conventional balloon was a Heinkel III of KG27 on 13 September 1940. Returning from a raid on Merseyside, the bomber struck a cable over Newport, Monmouthshire, plunging into a residential area. Two children were killed on the ground as well as three of the crew, only the pilot baling out.

A further Luftwaffe loss was another Heinkel III at South Shields on 16 February 1941. After catching a wing on a cable, the bomber dived into the ground. All five of the crew were killed, including one who baled-out but was unlucky enough to be electrocuted on trolley bus wires.

Of the British aircraft unfortunate enough to fall victim to the balloon barrage, at least some managed to survive the collisions. The Sheffield barrage saw at least two such incidents; a Hampden which crashed-landed in a public park in the city and a Wellington which limped back to base. Most incidents, however, were fatal with the aircraft being brought down in a spin from relatively low altitude, thus giving the crew no time to escape.

Towards the end of 1941, and with the reduced scale of attack, there was a change of policy with balloon barrages in view of the high accident rate to friendly aircraft. With improved communications and equipment increasing the speed at which close-hauled balloons could be raised in an emergency, so most provincial barrages were henceforth grounded except when hostile aircraft were known to be operating - although, despite these measures, there were still cable collisions.

By 1942, however, the grim tally of friendly aircraft was much reduced, although one of the worst accidents occurred over London on 6 October 1943, when a RAF Dakota struck two cables, ripping off one wing. Although the pilot tried to land in Regents Park, the aircraft became uncontrollable, the inevitable crash killing all nine on board.

However, on one occasion, several balloons broke free in a storm and

Facing Page Above This barrage balloon been readied for flight in central London gives a good impression of its size. The attachment points of the various cables can be clearly seen.
Facing Page Below Diagram of the Mk VIII K B Balloon showing its principal features.
Left Although the presence of barrage balloons could be a comfort to the general-public, they could be quite frightening to young children. To allay the fears of children, these two books were produced to present balloons as benign and friendly, with 'Boo-Boo' and 'Blossom' being popular bedtime stories during the Blitz.
Above Right The involvement of WAAFs on balloon duties was announced on this front cover of the popular wartime magazine, Picture Post.
Right Dame Laura Knight's painting of WAAF personnel handling a balloon at Coventry is illustrative of the hard physical work involved on balloon squadrons.

drifted across the North Sea, trailing their cables across occupied Europe and into Germany. The devastation was enormous as the trailing cables fouled power lines. This resulted in the birth of the long-running 'Operation Outward Bound' – a scheme whereby another type of balloon with long trailing cables were deliberately and regularly released into prevailing westerly winds, thus wreaking a degree of havoc on German war efforts. The storm which caused the accidental release of those initial balloons was certainly an 'ill wind' for Germany!

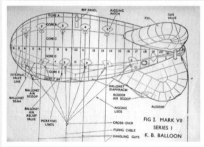

THE BALLOON

Each Barrage Balloon was 62 ft long and around 25 ft in diameter and made up of 24 panels from bow to stern. Every panel was of an exact size and fabric workers had to sew and glue the seams together to construct the balloon, the material being a silvery-grey rubberised fabric. The construction process meant inhaling fumes from benzene-based solvent and workers were given an extra pint of milk a day to protect them from the effects of the materials in use. One of the most important factories making balloons was at Kelvin Hall, Glasgow, where many thousands were produced.

The balloon had a capacity of 20,000 cu ft of hydrogen, but the lower one-third (called a ballonet) was not filled with gas but with air from a scoop on the underside, near the bow. Between the upper and lower compartment was a sheet of balloon fabric, the principle being that as the balloon rose, so its hydrogen expanded. To prevent the balloon bursting, this diaphragm was forced down into the ballonet which then vented to the air. In this way, the balloon did not appear to change shape as it expanded itself down into the air-filled ballonet. At the rear of the balloon were three 'fins' filled with air from the scoops. When inflated, the fins maintained the balloon's heading into wind and gave stability. Five rigging patches were used to attach picketing lines attached to handling guys to enable the balloon to be handled on the ground. When bedded down, the picketing lines were securely fastened to large concrete blocks set out in diamond shapes. Alternatively, the picketing lines were attached to screw pickets like huge metal corkscrews twisted into the ground. Six similar patches were used for the

rigging lines and were known as 'ton patches' as they supposedly could withstand a weight pull of one ton. Each patch was positioned at precise points along the balloon and each rigging line was of an exact length enabling the cables to meet at a single point under the balloon, meaning the upward force of the balloon was distributed along these cables which met at a point known as the crossover. In practice, this meant the balloon flew slightly nose down. At the crossover, the main flying cable was connected, this cable leading down to the winch. It was the suspension of this steel cable which was the sole purpose of the balloon.

The balloon also had a 'rip-panel' which was securely glued to the fabric. Underneath was a hole in the envelope, and between the balloon and the rip-panel was a strand of very sharp cheese wire attached to a red cord. Pulling on this caused the wire to slice through the rip panel, venting the hydrogen. Thus, in an emergency, the rip panel was pulled to deflate the balloon to prevent it running amok in bad weather.

Above Right Hajo Hermann in the cockpit of his Junkers 88 of KG 30 during 1940. **Below Right** Hauptmann Hajo Hermann pictured in an original colour wartime photograph.

HEYDAY OF THE BALLOON

Defensive balloons came into their own during 1944 when the VI Flying Bomb offensive began, with the original deployment utilising a belt from high ground between Cobham in Kent and Limpsfield, Surrey, and kept permanently airborne. The strength of the belt was doubled by drawing on other barrages from around the country.

By the beginning of July 1944, a thousand balloons were in position and arrangements made to add a further 750 so the barrage could be extended slightly to the west and increased in density.

On 28 August 1944, guns, fighters and balloons destroyed 65, 23 and two VIs respectively. Of the 97 that approached London that day, only four reached the city. When the VI onslaught ceased, an astonishing 231 flying bombs had been brought down by balloons. It was the heyday of the barrage balloon. However, their value quickly declined thereafter.

The Under-Secretary of State for Air, when asked in Parliament in October 1945, as to how many enemy aircraft had been destroyed by balloon cables replied:

'*24 piloted and 278 non-piloted. Unfortunately, 91 of our own aircraft collided with cables, causing 38 of them to crash.*'

In giving that figure, the government was being somewhat economical with the figures relating to RAF aircraft less than half the *actual* total. It seems that the number of enemy aircraft destroyed was similarly distorted. However, the deterrent value of the barrage balloon was incalculable, and they remain an abiding image of the Home Front.

The opening paragraph of Battle of Britain pilot Richard Hillary's '*The last Enemy*' paints a vivid picture:

"*September 3 dawned dark and overcast, with a slight breeze ruffling the waters of the Thames Estuary. Hornchurch aerodrome, twelve miles east of London, wore its usual morning pallor of yellow fog, lending an added air of grimness to the dimly silhouetted Spitfires around the boundary. From time to time, a balloon would poke its head grotesquely through the mist as though looking for possible victims before falling back like some tired monster.*"

It was an observation highlighting the true menace of the balloon barrage to friend and foe alike. ∎

ENCOUNTER OVER PLYMOUTH

Most aircraft which encountered barrage balloon cables in flight were almost certain to be destroyed, with survival from such an impact highly improbable. However, one Luftwaffe bomber crew operating over Britain had a remarkable and extremely lucky escape after 'landing' on top of a barrage balloon rather than striking its cable.

On the evening of 22 July 1940, four Junkers 88 aircraft of 7./KG 30 set out to drop magnetic mines into Plymouth Sound, led by Hauptmann Hajo Hermann. The operation would culminate in a low-level and low speed delivery of their loads in a heavily defended area. For Hermann and his crew, it would be an unforgettable mission. Approaching over the north-eastern outskirts of Plymouth, heading south-east at around 15,000 ft, Hermann throttled back and extended his dive brakes and trimmed the aircraft nose-up to achieve an almost flat, quiet, 45° descent onto the release zone. With the breakwater release point in sight, and searchlights stabbing the sky searching for them, the aircraft was now coming down to around 6,000 ft in bright moonlight, when suddenly a grey bulbous mass loomed directly in Hermann's path – a barrage balloon!

With no opportunity to take avoiding action, at slow speed and in a semi-stalled flying attitude and with the controls unresponsive, the Junkers literally wallowed onto the top of the balloon rather than flew into it. What happened next was described by Hermann as: '...like trying to fly a grand piano which had been thrown from a high-rise apartment!'

After seconds, the bomber fell off the balloon and the crew suddenly found the

searchlights still shining at them. Only now they were from above. They were tumbling earthwards, but upside down!

With the realisation they were still alive, Hermann shouted 'Aus!' to his crew, ordering them out of what seemed to be a stricken aircraft. A wall of cold air slammed into the cockpit as the canopy was released and Hermann selected full throttle and closed the dive brakes. Almost immediately, and just as the crew were about to abandon the Junkers 88, control was regained right above the breakwater. Releasing his mines, a shaken Hermann roared off at full throttle, chased by ground fire. Behind him, the flapping and deflating balloon descended over the city.

It had been an incredible escape - although had the Junkers 88 been just a few feet lower when it met the balloon, it would have impacted the cable head-on. The outcome, then, would have been rather different.

The Men : The Machines
The Battles : The Losses

The Men Stories of the pilots and aircrew
The Machines A spotlight on each aircraft type
The Battles Examination of individual battle days
The Losses The grim reality of the battle

'Put That Light Out!'

The defence of Britain during the Blitz and the aerial assault on the country was not just about active defences through weaponry. The passive defences provided by Air Raid Precautions were also crucial in defending the civilian population.

Government consideration for the protection of the civilian population in the event of air raids increased during the 1920s and 30s, largely born out of the experience of bombing by Zeppelins and Gotha bombers during the First World War when it became clearly apparent that civilians were now on the front line. That concern was heightened during the 1930s with the rise of tensions within Europe and the Spanish Civil War where the bombing of Guernica potently demonstrated a German ability and willingness to target civilians.

By April 1937, the Air Raid Warden's Service had been established to report on bombing incidents with the service expanded such that by January 1938 every local authority had to organise ARP wardens, messengers, ambulance drivers, rescue parties and set up liaison between the Police and Fire Brigades.

Across that period of the late 1930s, some 200,000 people had volunteered for the service. Then, during the Munich crisis of September 1938, another 500,000 had enrolled in what was a burgeoning and highly efficient organisation.

Perhaps indicative of the seriousness with which Britain viewed ARP measures were the popular series of cigarette cards produced by W D & H O Wills in 1938 which covered the subject of Air Raid Precautions.

These were described as 'Cigarette Cards of National Importance' on the collector's album cover.

Left The blackout was rigidly enforced by the ARP wardens. Here, for public information, a warden at Kingston sets the blackout time on an indicator clock.

LOOMING CONFLICT

As war loomed, there was a fear that poison gas might be deployed following the experience of gas attacks on the Western Front during the First World War. In the event, no such attacks against Britain materialised but a decision had been taken to equip every single person with a precautionary gas mask. This meant that approximately 40 million were required and it fell to the ARP service to help distribute and fit gas masks and to offer advice and instruction to the public. The wardens were also involved in the distribution of government leaflets advising how the public could protect themselves during air attacks.

Then, as war seemed inevitable and imminent, a nationwide 'blackout' was imposed at dusk with effect from 1 September 1939, its implementation being enforced by patrolling wardens who would shout the familiar *'Put that light out!'* at offending households. The purpose of the blackout was to prevent light showing from any premises which could have facilitated enemy bombers in their location of targets. The scheme required shutters or heavy curtains to block out any light and it was rigorously enforced. Persistent offenders who broke blackout rules were reported to the Police and prosecutions were not uncommon.

Then, on 3 September, the outbreak of war put the ARP services on a rather more serious footing.

HIGHLY DANGEROUS ROLE

Although standard procedures prescribed that the ideal warden should be at least 30 years old, men and women of all ages became wardens. The role of an ARP volunteer was open to both men and women, but only men could serve in the gas contamination, heavy and light rescue and demolition services.

Control of a local authority warden service was via a Chief Warden to whom each sector's area warden would report. Within metropolitan boroughs, the aim was to have one warden for every 500 residents, reporting from individual warden posts – each with its own post warden. Post wardens received messages from local wardens which they passed to a central Report and Control HQ.

Initially, ARP wardens were set up in temporary posts such as homes, shops and offices and only later in purpose-

Top With the worry that poison gas might be deployed, one of the first wartime duties of the ARP wardens was in the issue of gas masks to every civilian in Britain.

Above Many women served with the ARP organisation, including Barbara Nixon who was one of the first women to serve as a full-time warden in London.

Above Left Public interest in matters relating to protection during air raids heightened during the Munich crisis of 1938, but then took on even greater significance with the outbreak of war. Official and unofficial publications told the public what they should do, including this booklet with its dramatic cover. For the princely sum of sixpence, it told worried civilians how to protect themselves.

Left Recruitment into the ARP saw 1.5 million men and women volunteer for service.

THE ARP SERVICE

The role of those who served within Air Raid Precautions (later the Civil Defence Service) broadly spanned the range of duties set out below:

Wardens ARP wardens ensured the blackout was observed, sounded air raid sirens, safely guided people into public air raid shelters, issued and checked gas masks, evacuated areas around unexploded bombs, rescued people where possible from bomb damaged properties, located temporary accommodation for those who had been bombed out, and reported to their control centre about incidents, fires, etc. Also, they called in other services as required.

Report and Control Central headquarters that received information from wardens and messengers and managed the delivery of the relevant services needed to deal with each incident.

Messengers Often Boy Scouts or Boys' Brigade members aged between 14 and 18 acted as messengers or runners to take

verbal or written messages from air raid wardens and deliver them to either the sector post or the control centre. Bombing would sometimes cut telephone lines and messengers performed an important role in giving the ARP services a fuller picture of events.

First Aid Parties Trained to give first response first aid to those injured in bombing incidents.

Ambulance Drivers Casualties from bombing were taken to first aid posts or hospital by volunteer drivers. There were also stretcher parties that carried the injured to posts.

Rescue Services The rescue services were involved in getting the dead and injured out of bombed premises.

Gas Decontamination Specialists to deal with and clean up incidents involving chemical and gas weapons.

Fire Guards Following the destruction caused by the bombing of the City of London in late December 1940, the Fire

Watcher scheme was introduced in January 1941. All buildings in certain areas had to have a 24-hour watch kept and in the event of a fire the fire watchers could call on the rescue services and ensure they could access the building to deal with incidents. Note: All ARP service personnel were issued with standard British helmets, although Fire Watchers' helmets were of a different pattern. Depending on the role of the wearer, the helmet would be marked with a letter or letters to easily allow others to ascertain their role at an incident. These included:

W Wardens (some warden/fire guards had W/FG). Rank within the service was denoted by a white helmet and black bands.

R Rescue Services (later HR and LR were used for heavy and light rescue parties)

FAP First Aid Parties

SP Stretcher Parties (to carry injured from incidents)

A Ambulance Drivers

M Messenger/Runner

Left Anxiously scanning the sky for incoming raiders, a female ambulance driver sets out on another call. Slung over her shoulder is her service respirator in its haversack.

Far Right A documentary film called 'Fires were Started' told the story of the wartime fire service and used real firefighters rather than actors. This dramatic scene is a still from the film.

Right 'Heroes with grimy faces' was how Britain's firefighters came to be known. They featured here on the cover of 'Picture Post' during February 1941, at the height of the Blitz.

Below Right First Aid was an important function of the ARP organisation, with many injuries inevitably arising from air raids and often involving lacerations from flying glass.

THE FIRE SERVICE

An Auxiliary Fire Service (AFS) was first formed in 1938 in Great Britain as part of the overall civil defence structure, its role to supplement the work of fire brigades at local level. In this role it was hampered severely by the incompatibility of equipment used by different brigades – most importantly the lack of a standard size of hydrant valve.

The Auxiliary Fire Service and the local brigades were superseded in August 1941 by the National Fire Service (NFS) which standardised equipment and organisation. After the war, the AFS was reformed alongside the Civil Defence Corps, forming part of the UK's planned emergency response to a nuclear attack.

Members of the AFS were unpaid part-time volunteers but could be called up for whole-time paid service if necessary. This was similar to the wartime establishment of the Police Special Constabulary. Men and women could join, the latter mainly in administrative or messenger roles.

Not only were Britain's firefighters during the Second World War often dealing with extremely dangerous and challenging fires but they were frequently doing so under bombardment or in the presence of unexploded bombs. In total, 997 firefighters were killed during the war – 327 in London. And it was in London, after the attacks on 7 September 1940, that the vast majority of the city's members of the AFS saw their first blaze. It was literally a baptism of fire.

An enduring symbol of the fortitude and courage of London's firefighters during the Blitz is the image of St Paul's Cathedral (see page 130) rising above the flames on the night of 29 December 1940.

As with other members of Britain's civil defence organisation (and not forgetting the Police forces), many AFS or NFS members across the country received high awards for bravery.

built facilities. In cities, a warden's post was responsible for a smaller area than in rural areas, with five wardens to every 4–5,000 people. In London, there were approximately ten posts per square mile. Divided into sectors, each post had between three and six wardens who had local knowledge of the location of shelters, utilities (water, gas, electric), what buildings contained (important for fire services) and who was resident in their sector and where they lived.

The role of ARP services came into their own during the Blitz of 1940–41 when the ARP control centres would initiate the sounding of air raid sirens and wardens would marshal people into public shelters and then watch out for the fall of any bombs within their sector – often done during air raids and therefore a highly dangerous role.

When wardens came across the site of a bombing they would telephone for emergency services, render first aid to victims with minor injuries and deal with small fires such as the placing of sand on incendiary devices. Other ARP units included first-aid, light and heavy rescue parties, stretcher parties and messenger boys who cycled between incidents carrying messages from wardens, or from control centres at times when telephone communications were disrupted.

Other duties included helping to police areas suffering bomb damage and in helping bombed out householders. They were also tasked with keeping an emergency under control until other official rescue services arrived on the scene.

CASUALTIES AND BRAVERY

A small number of ARP wardens were full-time and paid a weekly wage (£3 for men and £2 for women), but most were part-time volunteers. Part-time wardens were supposed to be on duty about three nights a week, increased when bombing was heavier. One in six were female, and among male volunteers were many who were too old to serve in the military.

From 1941, the ARP officially changed its title to the Civil Defence Service to reflect the wider range of roles it then encompassed.

Almost 7,000 Civil Defence workers were killed and many injured. In total, some 1.5 million served in the organisation and over 127,000 full-time personnel were involved at the height of the Blitz. By the end of 1943 this had fallen to 70,000.

A number of those who served received the George Cross, George Medal or other commendations for bravery or valuable service.

The Civil Defence Service was stood down towards the end of the war in Europe on 2 May 1945, but the Cold War saw the service resurrected in the form of the Civil Defence Corps between 1949 and 1968. ∎

'Take Cover!'

For many, air raid shelter life was a familiar feature of the Blitz and during other periods of sustained aerial bombardment, particularly in cities and the larger towns. How and where the population took shelter varied enormously.

Photographs of civilians taking shelter in London Underground stations are some of the most iconic and memorably enduring images of the Blitz. As with the Zeppelin and aircraft raids of the First World War, Londoners flocked to the underground stations to seek what protection they could from air attack. Deep underground, of course, was the most obvious place to seek protection. But it was not always the safest place.

With the initial absence of any large public shelters, Londoners felt the only solution to ensure safety was to seek refuge in tube stations, especially when the Blitz got underway on 7 September 1940. From then on, right around to the following spring, many residents of the city flocked to the stations nightly and slept on the platforms. It was uncomfortable and not exactly restful. Not only that, but it was unsanitary because tube stations had no toilet facilities or water supplies.

DEADLY SHELTERS

The government had already taken the view that it did not wish to see tube stations being used as deep shelters, fearing that once people entered them, they would be reluctant to come back above ground and continue normal life. Of course, that did not happen. It would potentially be disruptive to essential travel too.

However, before the Blitz began, the government ordered London Transport not to allow the public to use stations as shelters. Underground station staff found, however, that it was completely impossible to stop people entering and setting up their own primitive camps below ground. Nevertheless, the stations did not necessarily offer the protection

Facing Page These Londoners look content in what they believe to be the safety of the London Underground station at Bounds Green during the early days of the Blitz. It remains an enduringly iconic image from the Blitz, but a tragic story lies behind the photograph as it was Bounds Green Underground station which took a direct hit from a German bomb on 8 October 1940, killing 19 people and injuring another 52. Quite likely, some of those victims appear in this photograph.

Top The extent to which Underground stations were used as shelters during the Blitz is wonderfully illustrated by this photograph at Aldwych. The line had been taken out of service on 22 September 1940, and so the sight of people sleeping on the tracks is not as alarming as it would first appear.

Above Left The same spot at Aldwych today, with the station remaining closed.

Above Right War artist Joseph Bato painted this scene from the Blitz during 1941 on the steps leading down to Queensway Underground station.

Above Putting a brave face on things, entertainment became a feature of shelter life. There was even an air raid shelter song!

Above Right Eventually, and despite the inherent unsuitability of the Underground as a place of refuge during air raids, London Transport relented and allowed the public to come into the tube system for shelter.

which those seeking shelter had naturally assumed. Sometimes, they were deadly. Nightly, though, the stations were filled and the greatest number of people in the Underground on any one night has been estimated as 177,000 on 27 September 1940. It was a sizeable figure, but only represents approximately 5% of London's wartime population.

A high explosive bomb, though, could penetrate deep into solid ground, and when a bomb scored a direct hit on the Marble Arch subway 17 September 1940, the subway was filled with people sheltering. Unfortunately, the blast ripped the white ceramic tiles from the walls as the bomb burst and turned shards of tile into deadly projectiles. Twenty people were killed.

Then, on 7 October, seven people were killed and another 33 others injured, at Trafalgar Square station when an explosion caused the concrete and steel casing over an escalator to collapse. The next day, 19 were killed and 52 injured at Bounds Green station.

The most destructive incident caused by a bomb on one of the stations, though, was on 14 October 1940. This was at Balham, when a large fragmentation bomb fell on the road above the northern end of the platform tunnels, creating a large crater in the road into which a double decker bus then crashed. The northbound platform tunnel partially collapsed, the remains of the tunnel filling with earth as well as water from the fractured water mains and sewers running above.

Although more than 400 people managed to escape, 68 died in the disaster, including the stationmaster, a ticket-office clerk and two porters. Many of the victims drowned as water and sewage from burst pipes poured in, soon reaching a depth of several feet.

CONFUSION AND PANIC

The deadly toll continued when, on 11 January 1941, a bomb penetrated the roadway and exploded in Bank Underground Station, killing 51 people. One of those who survived was Thomas Sergeant who recalled:

'I actually escaped obliteration myself by about one minute, since, in company with a Hungarian doctor whom I had met on the train on the way up from Sevenoaks, I had just got into Bank station and down on the Central Line platform before the bomb fell into the booking hall. What happened there I only know of second-hand. We were amongst those caught on the Central Line platform. The explosion was pretty fierce, the lights went out and the air was so thick with dust that torches were of little use. Most of those sleeping at the bottom of the escalator seemed to have been killed outright, as well as one or two on the platform. Just outside a few yards from where we were standing a large number were hurt by falling debris and tiles, or so it appeared in the dark.'

It was a grim toll, but worse was to come on the night of 3rd March 1943. Then, an air-raid warning sounded, and locals raced for cover at Bethnal Green tube station. Confusion and panic conspired to trap hundreds on the staircase entrance, and it is thought than further panic ensued when a nearby anti-

Above This was the scene of the tragedy at Balham when a bomb penetrated the road on 14 October 1940 and exploded in the Underground station below, killing 68 people. A London bus then fell into the huge crater.
Right The scene inside one of the tunnels at Balham.

aircraft battery opened fire. It is believed that one person then tripped and fell, and in the crush that followed, 173 were killed, including 62 children. More than 60 people were injured. Ironically, no bombs were dropped during the air raid alert which had triggered the disaster.

Nevertheless, and despite these tragedies, a certain young politician named Barbara Castle (who would later rise to high government office) wrote positively of the London Underground shelters during the earlier days of the Blitz:

'When the Blitz came, the people of London created their own deep shelters: the London Underground. Night after night, just before the sirens sounded, thousands trooped down in orderly fashion into the nearest Underground station, taking their bedding with them, flasks of hot tea, snacks, packs of cards and magazines. People soon got their regular places and set up little troglodyte communities where they could relax. I joined them one night to see what it was like. It was not a way of life I wanted myself, but I could see what an important safety-valve it was. Without it, London life could not have carried on in the way it did.'

Psychologically, it was the case that Londoners felt safe there. Sadly, in many instances, that proved not to be so. However, other types of air raid protection were also available to members of the public.

THE ANDERSON SHELTER

The principal means of shelter for those who possessed a garden was the Anderson Shelter. A thick corrugated iron, six-section (three per side) arched structure, with two end pieces, it was the brainchild of William Peterson and Oscar Kerrison.

Designed in 1938 at the instigation of Sir John Anderson, then the Lord Privy Seal (and later Home Secretary) with responsibility for preparing Air Raid Precautions, the shelter was meant to be buried 4ft into the ground, leaving the top 2 ft exposed. This was then covered with a minimum of 15 inches of soil, the design giving it greater elasticity in a near miss and some protection from shell fragments and bomber splinters. It was never intended that it should give total protection and it would clearly not withstand near or direct hits. However, it did mean that householders were less likely to be trapped, killed or injured in collapsed houses. It was designed to accommodate up to six persons. Because the structure was better able to flex and dissipate blast, it was safer than a brick surface shelter which tended to collapse or be weakened sufficiently

to allow the concrete roof slab to fall in. The earth covering of an Anderson Shelter could be turfed or planted over to minimise the intrusion of war, this leading to some streets and neighbourhoods even holding competitions for the 'Best Planted Shelter'!

For those on low incomes (then decreed as £5 per week) the local authority would supply the shelter free of charge, otherwise a £7 charge (£390 today) was levied. Between February and September 1939, some one-and-a-half-million shelters had been built, with a total of 3.6 million at the end of the war. A major producer was John Summers & Sons of Shotten, Deeside, who turned out 50,000 units per week.

Although proving satisfactory in the early months of the war, by the winter of 1940 they were proving very unpopular due to the cold, damp conditions inside. This was worsened by condensation running down the steel walls and, in many cases, flooding if a sump could not be dug to take off excess water, or in the absence of a shelter pump.

The unattractive prospect of stumbling down a garden in the dark, once the air raid warning had sounded, only to endure a

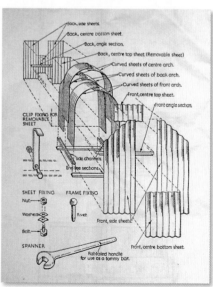

fitful night's sleep in the damp, and when the Luftwaffe sometimes didn't show up, led to many staying indoors in the warm and dry. This led to an inevitable increase in casualties.

A solution to this problem was found in 1941 with an indoor steel-framed, mesh-covered floor shelter called the Morrison Shelter.

Above These Londoners had a lucky escape in their Anderson Shelter when bombs exploded on the houses behind. Had they been in their homes they would probably have been killed or very seriously injured.

Facing Page Top Not exactly home comforts with all 'mod-cons', but this young couple and their children have settled down for the night in their Anderson Shelter. Despite their primitive nature, and being far from comfortable, their use saved a great many lives.

Facing Page Right Flat-Pack, 1940 style! The shelters were delivered in sections together with instructions and a spanner for construction.

WHEN THE SIREN SOUNDS...

Although many people took to some form of air raid shelter by night as a matter of course – especially during heightened periods of air attack – it was often the case that civilians would go to air raid shelters when the local air raid siren sounded.

Britain had two air raid warning alerts:

Red Warning: attack in progress or imminent (a warbling siren)

All Clear: attack over (a steady note from the siren)

The 'Red Warning' was sounded when enemy aircraft were detected by radar and deemed a threat to the immediate area. The system was controlled from HQ RAF Fighter Command who fed the alerts as appropriate to the areas threatened.

Every village, town, and city in Britain had a network of dual-tone sirens to warn of incoming air raids. The operation of the sirens was coordinated by a wire broadcast system via police stations. In towns and cities with a population of over 3,000, powered sirens were used, but in rural areas hand-operated sirens were often used.

Right Trench shelters were dug to provide rudimentary cover from blast and bomb splinters but provided no appreciable measure of safety if bombs fell nearby. On the contrary, they could be lethal. These children watch enemy aircraft high above them during the autumn of 1940 from a basic shelter trench, but public trench shelters were more elaborate affairs with timbered floors, sides and a roof covered over with soil.

THE MORRISON SHELTER

This was a shelter which could be installed in a downstairs room. Named after the then Home Secretary, Herbert Morrison, the design was 6 ft 6 inches long x 4 ft 2 inches wide, allowing for two adults to sleep side by side. It could double-up during the day as a dining table or sideboard, once covered with a suitable tablecloth or rug.

Prime Minister Winston Churchill personally tested the proposed design at 10 Downing Street before the initial order for half a million was placed. It immediately proved a popular alternative to the Anderson Shelter, despite the risk of being trapped within if the occupant's house suffered a direct hit. However, the design allowed for withstanding the weight of a typical-sized house collapsing on it – although those inside could expect to wait for rescue in often hazardous circumstances had water or gas mains been ruptured and fire broken out.

Right The Deep Level Shelters at Clapham South were quite elaborate affairs with dormitory sleeping arrangements, toilets, washing facilities, a canteen and medical centre.
Below Right An entry ticket for the Clapham South Deep Level Shelter.

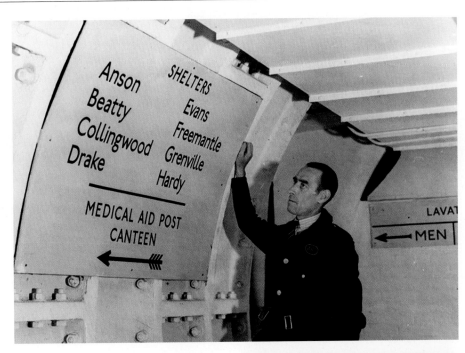

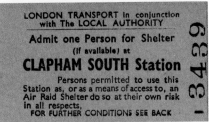

At the end of the war, both types of shelter were reclaimed for scrap if they had been supplied free of charge, but householders could keep them for a small fee. Thus, many Anderson Shelters lived on post-war to serve as useful sheds or wood stores - or two could be combined with straight sections down the middle to construct a garage.

Up and down the country there are still examples of Anderson Shelters soldiering on providing useful storage space, although the Morrison proved not to have the same degrees of peacetime versatility and is thus much rarer today. In rural areas, however, some survived as farmyard churn stands when milk was collected that way.

TRENCH SHELTERS
Essentially, these were exactly as the name describes them and were dug in parks and other public open spaces to afford some immediate protection to persons passing or in the vicinity from blast and bomb splinters, or for use by nearby residents who did not have Anderson Shelters.

The trench shelters dug in public parks were literally boarded-out trenches which also had a covered over timber 'roof' onto which the excavated soil was piled for added protection.

On the evening of 15th October 1940, however, a bomb fell on the Trench Shelter in Kennington Park, Lambeth, south London. It total, some 104 people were killed; the collapsing trench sides, and the board and earth 'roof', simply buried them alive.

Sadly, taking cover during an air raid was never any guarantee of safety. Sometimes, it proved lethal.

SURFACE SHELTERS
Surface shelters were often simply long brick-and-concrete structures built on pavements or beside buildings and in public areas. They had one or two entrances and offered immediate shelter from collapsing buildings and shrapnel. Some could hold several hundred people in varying levels of comfort, but they were not particularly blast-proof, however, as many were very badly constructed, often using sub-standard mortar, and liable to collapse. For the

most part, these surface shelters were of brick construction with a concrete slab roof.

Some other surface shelters were constructed from prefabricated reinforced-concrete units, and a few more bunker-like ones were cast *in situ* using shuttering.

The Civil Defence Act 1939 declared that: 'To lessen the number of casualties from a direct hit, the unit size of shelters should preferably be limited to parties of not more than 50 persons.' From then on, this became the common size for surface and semi-sunken air-raid shelters in schools, businesses, etc. Most were formed from pre-cast concrete panels or segments and could be built to different sizes and specifications.

DEEP LEVEL SHELTERS
None of the shelters described above could survive direct hits. Rather, as we have seen, they were designed to protect against the statistically higher possibility of a near miss, with its risk of flying bomb fragments and collapsing debris. In the pre-war period, however, there was a widespread campaign for the construction of deep underground shelters that could survive direct hits from heavy bombs.

Eventually, but not until the Blitz was underway, construction finally began in 1940 in response to a growing public demand for shelter in the London Underground. However, these shelters were not completed until 1942 after the main Blitz was over, so they were initially all used by government departments for other purposes.

Ten shelters were originally planned,

holding up to around 100,000 people in total across all shelters. However, the final capacity was around 8,000 people per shelter, and only eight were completed: at Chancery Lane station on the Central line and Belsize Park, Camden Town, Goodge Street, Stockwell, Clapham North, Clapham Common, and Clapham South on the Northern line. The other two were to be at St. Paul's station on the Central line (not built because of concerns about the stability of buildings above) and at Oval station on the Northern line which was not built because of difficult ground conditions encountered once work started. The working shaft for the shelter at Oval remains and now functions as a ventilation shaft for that station.

Each shelter comprised a pair of parallel tunnels 16 feet 6 inches (5.03 m) in diameter and 1,200 feet (370 m) long. Each tunnel was subdivided into two decks, and each shelter designed to hold around 8,000 people.

However, as bombing intensified again, five of the shelters were opened to the public in 1944: Stockwell, Clapham North, Camden Town, Belsize Park and Clapham South. The Goodge Street shelter was used by General Eisenhower as a HQ, and the Chancery Lane shelter as a communications centre. ■

Black Saturday

The Battle of Britain had rumbled on for three months when everything suddenly changed on Saturday 7 September 1940. On that day, London came directly under the Luftwaffe's full-scale air assault. The Blitz had properly begun.

Saturday, 7 September 1940, can be viewed as the day when the Luftwaffe had plainly lost its battle for air superiority over the RAF. To begin with on that day, however, there was considerable mystery as to what the Germans were up to. After all, the morning dawned fine with a light haze that soon cleared to produce a day that was near perfect for air operations. If the recent pattern were to be followed, then the Luftwaffe would shortly be mounting attacks on airfields in a manner that typified their recent operations.

As they nervously watched and waited, the commanders of the three main Fighter Groups in the south of England (10, 11 and 12 Groups) would ultimately be wrong-footed by the assumption that the attacks, when they came, would be against the airfields of RAF Fighter Command. Untypically, it was not until late afternoon that day that the attacks finally came.

16.15
The first formations of German aircraft were detected by radar, massing behind Cap Gris Nez. Shortly afterwards, more formations were picked up, one behind the other, approaching the south coast across a huge front. Inexorably, the massive aerial armada grew and advanced. In total, 348 bombers and 617 fighters swept towards England.

Reacting to the threat, Fighter Command scrambled three fighter squadrons towards the Thames Estuary and two more to patrol south of London. However, the Germans had taken considerable efforts to conceal the direction and intent of their attack. As such, London was not anticipated as the target by the RAF defenders. Those on the ground, just watching, were puzzled and alarmed. Farmer James Walker watched from his farm near Canterbury:

'I was rooted to the spot. At first it was like a swarm of midges high in the sky, at a distance. The low hum grew and grew as the specks got bigger and the hum became first a rumble, then a cacophonous roaring. It seemed an invincible force. Hundreds of them, stacked one on the other. I couldn't believe it. They just kept coming. And when I couldn't see any

Facing Page The second Great Fire of London. Framed by Tower Bridge, London's dockland is set ablaze during the late afternoon of Saturday 7 September 1940.
Right Although the direct attack on London came as a surprise to RAF Fighter Command, it also relieved the pressure on fighter airfields which had been coming under heavy attack. However, the front cover of this German magazine from 28 August 1940, Die Wehrmacht, perhaps illustrates the Luftwaffe's intentions.
Below Left London bound. Viewed from the cockpit of a Dornier 17-Z bomber, a formation advances en masse against London.
Below Right Viewed from another aircraft in the formation, two Dornier 17-Z bombers advance up the River Thames towards London.
Bottom Left Minutes later, bombs are falling on Tilbury Docks.

defending fighters, I thought: 'This is it. We've lost. We are going to be invaded today.' '

16.37

Fighter Command now reacted to the ever growing threat, committing 36 more fighters to the air from four squadrons. This was followed shortly after by eight more squadrons, as 12 Group in East Anglia were asked to send squadrons to supplement the bulk from 11 Group in the southeast. No less than 23 detachments from different squadrons were now airborne, but Fighter Command remained unsure as to German intentions. Cautiously, the controllers kept squadrons in defensive positions to cover the most likely targets: airfields.

On the plotting table at the HQ of 11 Group the staff watched in amazement as the counters steadily advanced. One WAAF, ACW Joan Harrington, recalled:

'I'd seen nothing like it before. I was almost running out of some of the map counters and keeping up with the plots took a lot of concentration. It had been so quiet that morning that I started to think this must just be an exercise, only nobody had told us. It didn't seem possible the Germans could be throwing this much at us. At least, not all at once!'

17.00

It was only now that battle began in earnest, and just as German intentions became obvious the first bombs began to fall on the eastern end of London around Woolwich. Gradually, the target area spread westwards, but eventually concentrated around the docklands area from about 17.15 hours setting much of

Top Left Further east down the Thames, an oil storage depot at Thameshaven is set ablaze.

Top Right The view across Fleet Street as the blaze in London's dockland area takes hold during the late afternoon of 7 September 1940.

Middle Right On 7 September 1940, Reichsmarschall Herman Goring, Chief of the Luftwaffe, arrived on the French channel coast to personally oversee the assault on Britain.

Above Reichsmarschall Herman Goring.

Left A dramatic artist's impression of a wall collapsing on two Firemen in Shoe Lane, London, during the height of the Blitz.

Above By nightfall on 7 September, when this photograph was taken, the Surrey Docks were well ablaze. The inferno was a beacon which guided more bombers to their target throughout the night.
Right The huge scale of the fires in London's dockland on 7 September tested the ability of firefighters to deal with the inferno. Availability of water supplies was often hampered when mains were hit and pumping water from the Thames became an issue because of the low tide. Meanwhile, as they fought the fires they were also braving further bombs.

the area to the east of Tower Bridge alight in one giant and growing inferno.

RAF squadrons had begun to engage, but for the most part were 5,000 feet below the enemy and their climb to engage lost the element of surprise. Running battles and chases, mostly with withdrawing enemy forces, began to spread out over Kent and Essex and southwards towards the Channel. Here, more than a few Messerschmitt 109 pilots ended their combat that day.

One, Hauptmann Heinz Bär of JG51, had been shot down into the sea a few days earlier. On 7 September, though, Hermann Göring arrived on the Channel coast to take personal charge of the air assault on London. Summoning Bär to tell him about his escapade, he asked what he had thought about while he was in the water. No doubt emboldened by his survival, and bemused by the

corpulent Göring's ridiculous appearance in his gold-trimmed pale blue uniform, Bär replied:
'Your speech, Herr Reichmarschall – reminding us that England isn't an island anymore!'

17.15
As battle was joined over east London, further plots of enemy aircraft were picked up by radar crossing the French coast. This time, two further squadrons were brought in to intercept; 43 Squadron with their Hurricanes and 602 Squadron's Spitfires.
Furious engagements ensued across Kent and up to the outskirts of London, and although the RAF fighters had considerable success there were also losses.

On 43 Squadron, the CO, Squadron Leader Caesar Hull, was shot down at Purley although his blazing Hurricane had hit the ground with such ferocity, and burned so furiously, that he could only be identified through the numbers on his aircraft's guns. Other pilots simply disappeared in the confusion of battle and were never seen again, no trace of them ever being found.

For 602 Squadron's CO, Squadron Leader 'Sandy' Johnstone, it was difficult to comprehend what he had seen:
'We nearly jumped out of our cockpits when we emerged from the haze. All we could see was row upon row of German raiders, all heading for London. I have

never seen so many aircraft in the air at one time for as far as the eye could see. The sky became a seething cauldron of vapour trails and tracer smoke, with aircraft weaving amongst it all. A Hurricane on fire spun down out of control, everyone was shouting at once and a Dornier spun down wildly with part of its port mainplane missing. A stoutly built German floated past me on his parachute, hands raised almost in surrender and, by now, fires were rising from huge fires along the River Thames. We had lost two of our pilots. It had been a black day, and the threat of invasion hung heavily.'

Right Sgt John McAdam was a Spitfire pilot with 41 Squadron and was involved in countering the Luftwaffe's assault during the late afternoon of 7 September 1940. He was shot down over Essex and had a lucky escape when his aircraft overturned and caught fire during a forced landing.

17.45

Still the German raiders came, and the attacks which ran from 17.45 until about 18.10 hours were the heaviest so far. The problem was that RAF Fighter Command had had many aircraft and squadrons airborne to engage the earlier and less important raid and had either engaged a retiring enemy or returned to their bases - or both. As a result, few of the later formations were engaged.

Additionally, at the end of the fighting that day, the wrecks of only two Luftwaffe bombers were found on land as opposed to fourteen enemy fighters. This reflected the nature of the fighting where the RAF defenders had primarily been involved with the fighters rather than the bombers. To a large extent, the escorting fighters had done their job and only 303 (Polish) Squadron enjoyed the ability to attack the bombers without being seriously interfered with by their escorts.

One of the squadrons engaged that evening was the Spitfire-equipped 41 Squadron from RAF Hornchurch. One of its pilots, Irishman Sgt John Mc Adam, was shot down and crashed near Rayleigh in Essex. Trapped in his overturned and burning Spitfire, McAdam later wrote matter-of-factly to his family of the ordeal:

'I was upside down and the cockpit was jammed, and the Spitfire was now burning, with flame and smoke building. I was about to pull out my revolver to end it all when I saw somebody through all the smoke. He had a big axe and smashed a way out for me. Otherwise, I'd have been done for. I got clear just in the nick of time.'

20.10

Although it was not yet dark, a further 318 bombers advanced, unescorted, up the Thames towards the fires still raging in the dockland area. Bluntly, the Air Ministry's own post-war history of the Battle of Britain stated:

'No attempt was made to intercept them, although darkness had not yet settled in.'

Why is not clear, although from 17.20 hours radar stations stopped giving any estimates of the raid size and yet the raids were detected, and patrolling RAF squadrons were airborne! However, the fact remained that this was just the start of wave upon wave of bombers which

would pound the Capital until 04.30 hours the next morning.

The fires were formidable and given that Fire Brigades measure a blaze by the number of pumps committed, so a 30-pump fire is regarded as 'very large'. At the height of the inferno, nine fires of 100 pump size were burning - the fire in Surrey Docks was the largest to ever occur in Britain. Further down the Thames, too, huge fires burnt at oil storage depots.

Of that night, one London Fireman spoke of being able to read a newspaper, miles away, and without a light. The German raiders thus had no trouble navigating to the target. On the ground, fire crews were dying and being injured.

One crew reaching a bombed building had rushed inside, as Sub Officer Harry Webb recalled:

'Wally shouted: 'You take the back, Harry, I'll look after this side' and I ran out intending to fight the fire from the rear when the whole bloody guts of the building fell in, burying the lot. We tore at a huge concrete slab that buried our mates, but it was hopeless. They were beyond aid, anyway.'

Saturday 7 September 1940 saw one of the darkest days and nights of the war thus far. It was also the day when an 'Invasion Imminent' signal was flashed to all three services. The reality, though, was that invasion was far from 'imminent' – although the Blitz had very much begun. ∎

Above The morning after. This iconic photograph of a milkman picking his way through the rubble was staged for the photographer but was intended to portray a resolute London carrying on in the face of adversity. After 7 September 1940, Londoners had to endure another eight months and five days of air attack. Gradually, the daylight raids petered out, but the night raids were almost continuous across that entire period.

Left Prime Minister Winston Churchill surveys the ruins in London's dock area the morning after the first big raid of the Blitz.

Britain's Blitzed Cities

Across Britain, every major city and many large towns came under ruthless enemy air attack during the main period of the Blitz. It wasn't just London which took the brunt of the Luftwaffe's intense bombing campaign.

The Blitz is often thought of as simply the intense Luftwaffe air attacks on London between 7 September 1940 and 11 May 1941. Whilst that is generally the understanding of this terminology, the reality was that most major cities the length and breadth of the British Isles came under attack across that period. As seen throughout this publication (detailed in the timeline, pages 14 - 15), Britain was 'Blitzed' to one degree or another between October 1939 and March 1945. Here, we highlight some of the many air attacks against Britain's other major cities.

Right Two boys pick their way through the rubble after a raid on Glasgow in March 1941 when the Clydebank area suffered terrible loss of life with 1,200 dead, 1,000 seriously injured and hundreds injured. Over 35,000 people were made homeless.

Left What became known as Sheffield's Blitz took place over the nights of 12 and 15 December 1940 and saw around 355 tons of high explosive and incendiary devices rained on the city. Sheffield was then a city of about 560,000 people and contained many heavy industries, primarily centred around steel and armament production. Thus, it was an important city on the Luftwaffe's target list, with Sheffield's Hadfield's steelworks the only place in Britain where 18-inch armour-piercing shells were being manufactured. In this image, a burned-out tram is silhouetted against the blazing city centre.

Right As Britain's second city, Birmingham was heavily raided on numerous occasions and eight time during the period 7 September 1940 to 11 May 1941. Here, firemen damp-down debris at The Bull Ring after one of the April 1941 raids.

Above Hull was struck three times during the Blitz period and significant damage was caused. The docks were a specific target. Here, the devastated British Oil & Cake Mills warehouse burns in Hull Docks.

Above Left Southampton was also badly hit, this being the aftermath when fighter-bombers struck on 15 September 1940. The target was Supermarine's factory where Spitfires were being constructed but the raiders could not find their objective and the bombs fell across residential areas. This was the aftermath at Woolston Railway Station.

Left Belfast, with its ship building industry, was also on the Luftwaffe target list as an important objective and was hit very heavily on two occasions during the main Blitz period. The clear-up and rescue efforts are shown underway after a Luftmine flattened a swathe of properties in a residential area. The tattered parachute from the mine is draped across the tram powerlines.

Above Left The most infamous attack of the Blitz was on Coventry on 14/15 November 1940. The city centre was badly hit and around 568 people were killed and 1,202 injured. The raid reached new levels of bombing intensity and Coventry Cathedral was destroyed and left as a permanent monument to the suffering of the Blitz. Here, Prime Minister Winston Churchill inspects its ruins with the city's Mayor, Alfred Grindlay.

Most Raided Town

Although London and other large provincial towns and cities were the main targets for the Luftwaffe, smaller towns also came in for attention. Among them, the Sussex seaside town of Eastbourne took a particularly heavy battering.

With its 112 air raids, 174 fatalities, 443 people seriously injured, 483 slightly hurt, 475 houses destroyed, 1,000 properties seriously damaged and another 10,000 slightly damaged, Eastbourne had the dubious 'claim to fame' as the most raided town in the south east.

In his despatch on Anti-Aircraft Command, General Sir Frederick Pile confirmed that Hastings and Eastbourne suffered the worst in the raids against coastal towns, during attacks which saw almost 700 bombs of up to 1,000kg and other missiles - from incendiaries to V1 and V2 weapons - falling on Eastbourne's beleaguered population. As for Hastings, with a total of 85 enemy attacks, the town fell behind Eastbourne in this unenviable 'league table'. However, the so-called

Tip and Run attacks of 1942 and 1943 were what most jangled the nerves of Eastbourne's townsfolk.

Coming without warning, or sometimes after the 'all-clear' had sounded, the raids were dramatic and saw groups of fighter-bombers sweep in from almost sea level, delivering their bombs amid cannon and machine gun fire and then being gone in moments. They were also costly in terms of lives lost and properties damaged - but not always without cost to the Luftwaffe, either.

CANNON & MACHINE GUN FIRE

At around 13.50 hrs on Monday 4 May 1942, Eastbourne got its first taste of the Tip & Run raider's established tactics as nine Messerschmitt 109 F fighter-bombers swept in at no more than 100ft over the seafront, crossed the western

end of the town, roared over Beachy Head Road, banked tightly eastwards, and headed back out to sea. En-route, the Messerschmitts released nine 250 kg bombs, the first hitting St John's Church in St John's Road. Here, the bomb exploded in the organ loft, demolished the north chapel and set ablaze the roof as well as the clergy and choir vestries. The raging fire eventually spread to the spire, finally engulfing the entire church.

With stunning rapidity, another eight bombs exploded across the town. Variously, these fell on the main gasometer at Eastbourne Gasworks, on Number 1 platform at the railway station, on Fremlins Brewers, on the railway line near Cavendish Bridge and at the coal wharf. Also, one hit the east wing of the Cavendish Hotel, demolished three houses in Willingdon Road and hit the

Facing Page Eastbourne Railway Station was badly hit on several occasions. This was the aftermath of an attack on 14 March 1943.

Right and Far Right Life went on, despite the Blitz. Here, a couple are married in the air raid shelter beneath All Saints Church, Eastbourne, only emerging for their delayed wedding reception once the 'All Clear' had sounded.

Above In September 1939, the town's population of children was evacuated via Eastbourne Railway Station as a precautionary measure. As the war went on, many returned to the town – albeit that Eastbourne was becoming a far from safe place for them to be.

Top Right As the danger of attacks increased, the Eastbourne Police issued these information flyers instructing the population what to do in the event of air attack.

railway engine sheds. Apart from the fire at St John's Church, fires elsewhere meant that the fire service was hard-pressed to deal with all the calls for help. It would not be long, though, before the town's NFS themselves became victims of a Tip and Run attack.

Despite the destruction at the Cavendish Hotel, casualties were remarkably light - especially considering occupancy by the RAF who had requisitioned it for its No.1 Elementary Air Navigation School. Here, ACW Evelyn Stretton and AC Christopher Robinson were killed, along with civilians Winifred Matthews and Mary Richardson. On the outside of the hotel, repaired damage from bomb splinters can still be seen in the portico pillars of the main entrance – unique 'visiting cards' left by unwelcome visitors.

As with the Devonshire Hotel, the fatality list was remarkably light considering the spread of bombs and extensive damage to commercial and residential property. At the railway station, Claude Benjamin was fatally injured and at Willingdon Road, 84-year-old Anne Wise was killed in her bedroom. Thirty-seven others were injured, including service personnel. As the raiders sped out over the sea, fishermen Alec Andrews and Jesse Huggett were going about their business when their boat was raked with cannon and machine gun fire, wounding Andrews in the abdomen and leg and causing Huggett bullet wounds to his head, arms and legs. Over inside two minutes, it was a potent example of how dangerous the Tip and Run raiders could be. For Eastbourne, there would be much more of the same to come.

GIGANTIC FIREBALL

Just three days later, on 7 May, it became apparent to residents of Eastbourne that Tip and Run attacks by low flying and fast fighter-bombers might be a continuing feature as four more raiders swept across town. This time, during late afternoon, two pairs of Messerschmitt 109s approached from the west at 500

ft, dropping their 250 kg bombs as they headed out to sea. The bombs hit Victoria Place, demolishing three properties, and one more fell (again) on the coal wharf and another at the goods yard. The fourth fell harmlessly on the foreshore opposite the Hydro Hotel where the only 'military' damage was the demolition of several yards of defensive barbed wire. At the coal wharf, 36-year-old Home Guardsman and railway worker, Jack Payne, was killed as he cleared up debris from the 4 May raid. He was the only fatality, although 31 were injured, some seriously. Among the injured were Christopher Wilcock and Albert Reeve, crew members on the RN patrol vessel HMS *Pigeon*, shot up off Eastbourne by the departing Messerschmitts in an echo of the raid three days earlier.

For the town's residents, a pattern was now established: low level attacks off the sea, no warning, heavy calibre bombs dropped randomly, machine gunning of the town and any offshore craft attacked by the departing aircraft. Before long, though, there would be success in downing raiders attacking Eastbourne - but the town had yet to endure one more Tip and Run attack before any such success would lift local spirits.

At 05.50 hrs on 13 August 1942, four Focke-Wulf 190 aircraft streaked in from the east in two pairs of two. The aircraft arrived over the coast near Bexhill, heading west towards Eastbourne at no more than 30 ft. A Ministry of Home Security report later recording that the aircraft 'rose to clear telephone wires.'

The first pair dropped bombs at Pevensey Bay, with one striking a newsagent's roof and bouncing into Messrs Bambridge's garage where it exploded. The destruction was considerable, but there were no fatalities. Meanwhile, the second pair raced on to Eastbourne where two bombs were aimed at the Gasworks. Here, one bomb struck No.5 gas holder, penetrated the steel plate and exploded inside where it ignited 500,000 cubic feet of gas in a gigantic fireball and destroying the holder as its steel frame buckled and collapsed in on itself. The second bomb exploded in the garden of a house, causing considerable damage to nearby houses.

By good fortune, the raid only resulted in casualties and no fatalities but gas worker John H Colbran suffered broken ribs and a damaged right hand when he was crushed between the gasholder and a falling girder. The Chief Constable of Eastbourne, though, had a fortunate escape during the raid when a cannon shell smashed his office window in the Police Station at Grove Road before ricocheting around inside. Two weeks later, the tables would be turned on the raiders - albeit that significant havoc was caused during the raid of Wednesday 26 August 1942.

ROOFTOP GUNNERS

Shortly before 9 o'clock that day, a pair of low-level Focke-Wulf 190 aircraft of 10./JG 26 streaked in over the beach at Pevensey Bay, firing with machine gun and cannon as they passed. This time, seafaring folk were fired on as the aircraft came in on their attack run and 54-year-old fisherman, Alfred Grant, was hit by gunfire as he worked on the beach. Moments later, the raiders were over the eastern outskirts of Eastbourne, their target designated as: 'a factory area within a residential area'.

GIRL GUIDE 'VC'

Courage and fortitude shone like a beacon from the grim reality of Eastbourne's civilian population who had been thrust onto the front line. After one particularly dreadful air attack there were no less than 14 honours for courage – among them, four George Medals, one MBE and the exceptionally rare honour of the Girl Guides' Gilt Cross for Gallantry.

By Saturday 28 September 1940, the 'Blitz' proper had been in full swing for three weeks – but it was not only London that was taking a battering.

At around 6pm, two German bombers, pursued by a single Spitfire, swept across Eastbourne and released salvoes of high-explosive bombs around the area of the town's Cavendish Railway Bridge, Cavendish Place, Tideswell Road and Bourne Street. At Cavendish Place, shops and houses were demolished and several people were trapped under the rubble. Among them, 17-year-old Peggy Harland.

Almost immediately, rescue parties were on the scene and despite the presence of a UXB in the debris of a nearby garage, and the hazard caused by leaking gas, live electric cables, and cascading water from a burst main, they struggled for hours in dangerous and truly appalling conditions. The principal focus in their rescue effort, though, was an attempt to free Peggy Harland whose legs were trapped beneath heavy debris.

For an agonising 36 hours, rescuers toiled to release her, but it eventually became clear that the only way to get her out was to perform an emergency operation to amputate her legs.

Throughout much of her dreadful ordeal, Peggy remained conscious and cheerful, her demeanour and attitude earning the undying respect of her rescuers. Without doubt, her outstanding courage had been a constant source of encouragement in their harrowing work. Sadly, she died in hospital two days later, finally succumbing to her appalling injuries and shock.

Peggy, a Girl Guide, was posthumously awarded the Girl Guides' Gilt Cross for Gallantry, an extremely rare and unusual honour. It has sometimes been described as the 'Girl Guides' VC'.

Top The wreck of Werner Kassa's Focke-Wulf 190 after being shot down by light anti-aircraft fire at Eastbourne on 26 August 1942. Inverted, and with its wings torn off, the aircraft ended up in a ditch alongside the town's Lottbridge Drove. The pilot was killed outright in the crash.

Above Left The report into the shooting down of Immervoll's aircraft by the CO of Princess Patricia's Canadian Light Infantry. Successes like this were a huge morale boost to the population of Eastbourne.

Above Centre Unteroffizier Albert Immervoll also fell victim to Canadian gunners during an attack on Eastbourne, his aircraft plunging into the sea beneath the famous cliffs at Beachy Head.

Above Right One of the victorious gunners from the Canadian Seaforth Highlander's Regiment poses with his trophy, the swastika cut from the tail fin of Werner Kassa's aircraft.

Below Right Today, that same swastika panel is preserved at the regimental museum in Canada, a tangible reminder of Eastbourne's ordeal by fire.

Below Houses in the town's Havelock Road were among the properties hit during the devastating attack on 4 June 1943.
Bottom The Metropole and Balmoral Hotels on Eastbourne's seafront took the full force of a direct hit from one of the bombs dropped on 4 June 1943.
Right One of the 40mm Bofors guns which defended Eastbourne from air attack. This gun is situated on the South Downs above the town and is manned by Canadian soldiers.

Leading the pair was 28-year-old Oberfeldwebel Werner Kassa, his wingman Obergefreiter Wittmann. The pair headed straight towards the workshops of Messrs. Caffyns Ltd in Seaside, then turned over to war work producing bodies for army trucks, NFS vehicles, searchlight wagons etc. Given the spate of raids, and the war work undertaken there, it was deemed appropriate to site a light AA gun on the roof of the workshop offices and paint camouflage on the seaward-facing garage walls. The rooftop gunners were men of the Seaforth Highlanders of Canada, and as the raiders flashed overhead, Private E G Johnstone loosed off a burst at the leading aircraft. What happened next was over in seconds.

The 'factory within a residential area' was the nearby Eastbourne Corporation Electricity Works where the first bomb exploded in the furnace house, killing fitter Frank Moore outright. Considerable damage was caused to an adjacent cooling tower, with debris thrown across the nearby road into an electricity sub-station causing damage to cable insulators. The second bomb fell yards away in Marlow Avenue, destroying three houses and damaging two others. Here, Lucy Dann was found in a rear garden with terrible injuries from which she later succumbed. Nearby, Post Office worker William Chatfield had a remarkable escape as he painted the back of his house from a ladder, but his daughters Paula and Marjorie were slightly injured. However, their mother, Ruth, suffered severe injuries and died later in hospital. One minute after the bombs had fallen, the local air raid siren sounded. By this time, Wittmmann was already heading back across the Channel - albeit alone. Werner Kassa, his aircraft hit, was decapitated when his aircraft plunged inverted into a drainage ditch just a few hundred yards from Private Johnstone's position.

When Johnstone loosed off his Bren gun fire, though, War Reserve Constable Harry Etherington had a grandstand view:

"I saw two FW 190s come in from the sea from the direction of Langney Point. I saw two bombs dropped. One 'plane then turned right and came over the gasworks. A machine gun posted on the top of Caffyns works in Seaside opened fire and I saw bullets entering the machine. It faltered, then turned completely upside down and crashed into the ditch bordering Lottbridge Drove about fifty yards from me."

Although Etherington was clear about what he saw, others felt the crash may have been caused by blast from the bombs. Either way, it was a tonic for war weary Eastbourne residents – one of whom wrote to the local newspaper that same day, 26 August 1942, making a call for 'proper protection' from such attacks. Relentlessly, throughout the year and into the next, such attacks continued. Occasionally, though, the defences *did* get the better of the raiders.

WORST CASUALTY TOLL

On 23 January 1943, for instance, four Focke-Wulf 190s of 10./JG 26 were sent to bomb Hailsham, but instead found Polegate just to the north of Eastbourne where the bombing killed three. However, one of the retreating raiders took a direct hit fired from a gun on Beachy Head, exploded, and fell into the sea at nearby Cow Gap, killing Unteroffizier Alfred Immervoll.

Then, on 7 February 1943, another attack saw the NFS Fire Station at the back of the Library and Technical Institute in Grove Road hit – just yards from the railway station. The resulting explosion was devastating, demolishing the Fire Station, damaging the library and institute and killing six NFS personnel; five men and a woman. Additionally, six more NFS personnel

were seriously injured along with four other civilians. Surprisingly, none of the fire appliances were seriously damaged despite the destruction. As shocked NFS survivors, bloodied and dirt covered, clawed themselves from the wreckage they set about digging out their trapped colleagues.

The Tip and Run raids continued against Eastbourne, with another punishing assault on 7 March seeing 15 aircraft attacking the town. Again, a massed force of 10 raiders came back on the 3 April. This time, the worst casualty toll was inflicted when twelve bombs fell resulting in 35 dead and 99 injured. In one incident, at Spencer Road, a surface air raid shelter took a direct hit killing 14. If anything, the raids were getting more severe, involved more aircraft, caused more damage and inflicted heavier casualties than before.

Again, on 4 June 1943, 18 Focke-Wulf 190s of SKG 10 swept in from Beachy Head and descended, hedge hopping, down the eastward slope of the South Downs before delivering at least fourteen bombs across the town. Remarkably, and despite widespread damage, only seven fatalities were caused with 33 injured. At St Saviours Church, an unexploded bomb crashed between the pews and was later dealt with by a Bomb Disposal unit, thereby saving another Eastbourne

Top At Norman's Bay, in a field behind the hamlet's Star Inn, Oberleutnant Kurt Hevler tried to get his Focke-Wulf 190 down in a crash-landing after being hit by flak during the attack on Eastbourne of 4 June 1943. Hevler's aircraft overturned in the high-speed impact, killing him instantly.
Above The Air Raid Warden's Report form relating to the deadly bombing of Eastbourne's Fire Station.

'Let's Hit it Hard!'

The tale of a Messerschmitt 109 fighter-bomber brought down on Beachy Head reveals a fascinating story to illustrate that Tip and Run raids were often costly and dangerous for the Luftwaffe.

To the farm workers toiling at Black Robin Farm on Beachy Head, the distant whine of aero engines was nothing that unduly concerned them. It was Wednesday, 20 May 1942, and such things were almost an everyday occurrence. Even the distant 'crump' of bomb explosions attracted scant attention.

Moments later, however, a lone aircraft unexpectedly hopped over the cliff edge trailing a banner of white vapour as it headed towards them, before suddenly careering across a meadow on its belly, ending in an awkward pirouette and swirling clouds of dust.

Gingerly, the pilot heaved himself out of the cockpit and fired his pistol into the engine in what seemed to the astonished farm labourers to be nothing more than frustrated rage.

Earlier that morning, Hauptmann Plunser of the Messerschmitt 109-F equipped 10(Jabo)/JG26, detailed 23-year-old Unteroffizier Oswald Fischer to lead a two aircraft sortie against Brighton. As Fischer later recalled:

"We had not visited the area for some time. Few wanted to fly there because of the long stretch over water. I planned to go inland about 20 miles before we hit the harbour. All worked out fine – a low flight over the Channel and hedgehopping over the British countryside - and right into the harbour at Brighton [sic.] I saw a ship and told my wingman: 'Let's hit it hard!'

The flak sprayed like a firehose, lazy yellow streaks zipping towards us. But we made it and struck the ship with both bombs. As we exited, I got hit.

I could hear impacts, but everything seemed OK. As soon as we were over the

water my temperature shot up and I could smell coolant, so told my wingman to keep going in low flight towards our base. Meanwhile, I turned round and belly-landed in a field. I tried to blow it up, but my explosive charge would not go off. Thus, I became a POW. I regretted my fate, but it was better than drowning in the English Channel."

For Oswald Fischer, the war was over. But his Messerschmitt lived on awhile.

STRAFING COWS

In many ways, Fischer was already a lucky man. Having apparently so far survived an astonishing 46 operational flights against Britain, he was living on borrowed time. His interrogation threw up interesting details, noting him as having 'high morale' and being 'confident and very self-possessed'. The summary of what he revealed is fascinating and boastful:

"In the previous month, this pilot made 46 war flights against England when the targets had been Folkestone and Deal railway stations, Hawkinge aerodrome, a colliery near Deal, barracks at Dungeness and some ships off Brighton. One day, he carried out three *operations to Folkestone. Other targets included strafing cows, cyclists, buses and railway engines. The pilot claimed 16 victories, three while serving in Libya, and 13 over the English Channel. He was the holder of the Iron Cross First Class."*

Fischer told his interrogators he started with his wingman from St Omer to attack shipping and harbour installations at Newhaven (seven miles east of Brighton), flying at sea level. No mention was made of penetrating 20 miles inland, but he said that when circling Newhaven, they spotted shipping, including a 'corvette', to the south-west of the port and dived to attack. Fischer released his 250kg bomb towards a 'naval vessel', but it struck the water alongside and bounced over it – something contradicted when Oswald Fischer claimed, post-war, that both pilots' bombs had hit their target.

The 'shipping' which attracted the attention of the pilots was the former River Clyde steamer, SS *Davaar*, anchored alongside the entrance channel to Newhaven. 'Kept in steam', she was ready to be swung abeam and sunk as a blockship in the event of invasion. Already, *Davaar* had come in for Luftwaffe attention. For example, on 24 March 1942, enemy aircraft attacked and dropped three bombs which narrowly missed her. The vessel's 'in steam' status had doubtless led her attackers to believe she was something other than a hulk ready for sacrifice as a defensive measure. All the same, had *Davaar* been hit, she could well have swung about and blocked the port. And with the Dieppe raid due to be launched from Newhaven in August, then the sinking of *Davaar* might have had serious consequences.

As to the aircraft, Messerschmitt 109 F-4 was built in 1941, as Werk Nummer 7232 and delivered to 10(Jabo)/JG26. However, while the RAF were keen to repair and test fly 7232, a cylinder block had been damaged in the crash landing – damage possibly compounded when Fischer emptied his pistol into the engine compartment!

Finally, on 24 October 1942, it was repaired ready for flight with No.1426 (Enemy Aircraft) Flight.

The Messerschmitt was eventually painted in RAF colours but would retain the bomb symbol on its rear fuselage. Finally, the aircraft was damaged on 7 January 1944 and ultimately scrapped.

'Today we attacked Eastbourne with strong forces flying at low-level. We achieved considerable destruction. Certainly, the flak fired considerably better than usual, and I was hit by a 2cm shell behind the engine which went through the whole aircraft. Several instruments failed and a small splinter went into my leg. I had more than enough trouble to bring my 'kite' home in one piece.'

Leutnant Leopold Wenger, IV/SKG 10, June 1943.

church from destruction. Among the significant buildings hit was the already damaged Library and Technical Institute. This time, the damage to the impressive building was terminal. On the seafront, the Metropole and Balmoral Hotels were destroyed, with an anti-aircraft site also hit. The local AA gunners, though, were to have their revenge.

Firing on the raiders, a direct hit sent Oberleutnant Kurt Hevler's Focke-Wulf 190 down to crash behind the Star Inn, Normans Bay, killing the unfortunate pilot as the aircraft turned over whilst attempting a forced landing. As the other aircraft fled south, they were engaged by Spitfires of 41 Squadron, with two

pilots making claims for other raiders downed in the sea. There were, however, no other losses to the raiding force other than that sustained with the shooting down of Kurt Hevler. (*Note: the front cover illustration of this publication is an artistic representation of the attack on 4 June 1943 when Kurt Hevler was brought down*)

Two days later, on 6 June, another 14 Focke-Wulf 190s returned and scattered bombs across the town, causing further damage and killing seven civilians and several Military Policemen. As the raiders departed, they shot up the Royal Observer Corps post on Beachy Head but were pursued by three Spitfires which managed to shoot down one of the attackers. For Eastbourne, though, the worst of the Tip and Run attacks were over.

Quite apart from these Tip and Run raids, Eastbourne had also suffered many other attacks by day and by night and at least five enemy aircraft had been brought down within the borough boundaries which also saw a number of VI Flying Bomb incidents along with a V2 rocket which exploded in mid-air just to the north of the town.

The earliest raid was on 7 July 1940, the last (a VI detonation) on 14 August 1944.

The attacks detailed here were not by any means the full sum of such raids but illustrate the astonishing ordeal suffered by just one seaside town. General Pile's statement that Eastbourne was 'the most raided town' needs little further qualification. ∎

Facing Page Unteroffizier Oswald Fischer's Messerschmitt 109-F is examined by RAF intelligence personnel after its crash-landing at Black Robin Farm on Beachy Head on 20 May 1942.
Above Under new management: repaired, re-painted and flown by the RAF, this was Unteroffizier Oswald Fischer's aircraft on one of its test flights. It still retained its fuselage numeral and large white bomb emblem.

The Night Fighters

Britain's defence against air attack fell largely to RAF fighters, anti-aircraft guns and barrage balloons. The role of night fighters in countering the Blitz, though, was an important yet challenging one and met with varying degrees of success.

When the Luftwaffe abandoned daylight attacks against airfields, aircraft factories and other parts of Britain's defence infrastructure in September 1940, turning instead against London and other cities, it was, of course, a relief to a beleaguered RAF Fighter Command. And yet it was also a bittersweet moment; while pressure was off the fighter defences, those same defences stood almost powerless to stop the night attacks.

Part of the problem was that RAF Fighter Command had been geared-up as a day fighter force, with relatively scant attention paid to night defence. In any event, pre-war preparations for the air defence of Britain were predicated on the notion that enemy bombers would not be able to see their military targets by night. Similarly, defending fighter pilots would be unlikely to be able to see any attackers, either. Thus, relatively little emphasis was

placed on night-fighting development. All this, of course, did not foresee the advent of radar or mass night-time attacks on British cities.

The thinking of planners during the 1930s was that British fighters would simply need to defend against daylight attackers crossing the North Sea, flying from German bases. It was considered that these bombers would be unescorted because of the range. For that same reason, the Boulton Paul Defiant four-gun turret fighter was conceived as a 'bomber destroyer' to sail into undefended bomber streams and pick them off. None of this foresaw German bombers operating from bases in France and Belgium, with fighter escorts based right up on the Channel Coast.

GRIEVOUS LOSSES

In many respects, RAF Fighter Command were wrong-footed as to how it might be required to defend

Britain. Notwithstanding the excellent infrastructure supporting Fighter Command through the world's first integrated air defence command and control system, nocturnal defence considerations were almost fatally lacking.

For the Luftwaffe, which suffered grievous losses during the daylight phase of the Battle of Britain, round-the-clock attacks on London and other centres of population, beginning on 7 September 1940, highlighted one fact: losses of bombers by night (which did not require fighter escort) were significantly less than daylight losses. The Luftwaffe was very much aware that the RAF's night-fighting capability – much like its own – would be unable to effectively counter nocturnal assaults.

Initially, daylight attacks continued in tandem with night raids, but daylight sorties resulted in continued heavy bomber losses. Meanwhile,

Facing Page The crew of a Blenheim night fighter of 29 Squadron clamber aboard their aircraft for another night patrol during the late autumn of 1940.

Right A Hurricane taxies out for a 'Fighter Night' operation during the height of the 1940/41 Blitz. Unaided by airborne radar, pilots were expected to search the night sky in the hope of catching raiders.

Below Left The Boulton Paul Defiant was not a success as a day fighter during the Battle of Britain but was put to good use in the night fighter role in 1940, giving valuable service throughout the Blitz. Pictured is the sole surviving example of a Defiant aircraft, held by the RAF Museum, and in the markings of 307 (Polish) Squadron.

Below Right This recruitment poster exhorted young men to volunteer for RAF flying duties. The airman featured is Pilot Officer Peter Parrot who flew Hurricanes with 145 Squadron and was one of the pilots selected to sometimes fly 'Fighter Night' operations which he recalled as: 'Utterly terrifying. Far scarier than meeting the Luftwaffe – which I never did at night!'

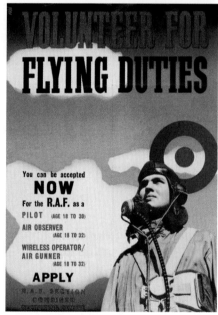

night bombers remained relatively immune from limited fighter defences and ineffective anti-aircraft guns. Unsurprisingly, mass daylight attacks had petered out by early October 1940.

STOPPING THE GAP

Despite the paucity of its night-fighting ability, the RAF recognised it needed to do more with what it had. Initially, and the few dedicated night-fighting squadrons aside, RAF Fighter Command committed day fighters to defensive patrols by night. Generally, these were by single Hurricanes or Spitfires sent off on patrol lines to search for raiders. Successes were minimal, although some early 'kills' were achieved even before the Battle of Britain had started, let alone the Blitz having commenced.

These early victories were achieved on the night of 19/20 June 1940, over East Anglia, when Spitfires of 19 and 74 Squadrons brought down three Heinkel 111s of Kampfgeschwader 4. They were, though, unusual successes. And night-fighter operations by single-seat fighters were hazardous as well as being generally unproductive, with a good many pilots lost on operations such as these. One was Sgt H N Howes, a Hurricane pilot with 85 Squadron.

An experienced fighter pilot in the Battles of France and Britain, Howes shot down at least ten enemy aircraft by day, shared in the destruction of others, claimed several damaged and others as

'probables'. Awarded the DFM, he was killed on 22 December 1940 after losing control during a futile 'Fighter Night' patrol. However, it had not all been about Spitfires and Hurricanes trying to 'stop the gap' by night.

On the same night as the success over East Anglia on 19/20 June 1940, Bristol Blenheims of 23 Squadron had joined the fray with one crew sharing in the destruction of one of the Heinkels hit by the Spitfires, and another crew shooting one down on the coast. But these crews had also relied on the 'Mk 1 eyeball' to find their quarry in the night sky.

NEW RADAR

Down on the Sussex coast, at RAF Ford, the newly formed Fighter Interception Unit, though, was developing night fighting techniques as well as initiating operations with new on-board A.I (Airborne Interception) Radar equipment.

On 23/24 July 1940 a Blenheim of the FIU made the first claim using the new equipment: a Dornier 17-Z over the English Channel. Some doubt, however, existed about the claim. To show that A.I worked, solid wreckage was needed on the ground, but that would be some

time coming. Quantitatively, though, the force of RAF night fighters was already theoretically strong enough to inflict serious losses on the raiders. Qualitatively, however, its equipment was poor and new technology insufficiently developed.

Meanwhile, stop-gap day fighters continued the battle. One or two, quite remarkably, achieved reasonable degrees of success on 'Cats-Eyes' patrols – using eyesight rather than radar. Also pressed into the night defence role were the Defiant squadrons. An abject failure against fighter-defended daylight bombers, they achieved reasonable success by night. The way forward, though, was to get A.I to the point of being an effective weapon and the

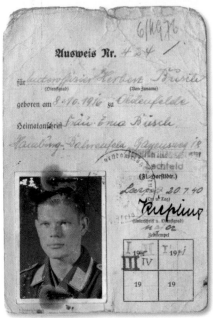

Top Left An RAF Intelligence Officer inspects the wreckage of a Junkers 88 as a young boy looks on. The aircraft was shot down at East Wittering, Sussex, on the night of 19/20 November 1940 by Flt Lt John Cunningham in an Airborne Interception radar equipped Beaufighter of 604 Squadron - the first confirmed 'kill' using the new airborne radar technology.
Top Right Night fighting was not without danger as evidenced by this scorched Mosquito of 410 (RCAF) Squadron which returned home after flying through an exploding Dornier 217 in September 1943.
Above The chances of being shot down at night were relatively low, but a good many bomber crews failed to return from operations over Britain. Unteroffizier Herbert Büsch, a Junkers 88 crew member with 6./KG 76, perished with two comrades when shot down by a Beaufighter of 604 Squadron on the night of 12/13 March 1941 during a night attack on Portsmouth. The aircraft crashed at Kingston Deverill, where Herbert Büsch's identity papers were found in the wreckage.

NIGHT INTRUDING

One of the aircraft types pressed into service in the night fighting role was the Douglas Havoc twin-engine aircraft with eight Browning .303 machine guns in the nose and a single .303 Vickers 'K' gun (seen here) mounted in the rear cockpit.

These aircraft were utilised for night intrusion work over France, Belgium and the Netherlands. The idea of these operations was to lurk around Luftwaffe bomber bases and to catch enemy aircraft either leaving for - or returning

from - sorties over the British Isles. This was rather than intercepting raiders which were already over or approaching mainland Britain. It was a role in which this aircraft type achieved some moderate success.

This particular aircraft, BB900, served with the RAF's 23 Squadron but was eventually lost on 27 February 1942 when it ditched in the sea off North Foreland. It has been roughly painted partly black for low visibility on nocturnal operations.

development of a Ground Controlled Interception system. Important, too, was the 'right' aircraft to fit the A.I into. Fortuitously, the Bristol Beaufighter was being brought into service in the night fighting role. And it was ideally suited for fitment with A.I.

Finally, on the night of 14/15 November 1940, Flight John Cunningham, in a Beaufighter of 604 Squadron, intercepted a Junkers 88 of I./KG54 over the West Sussex coast after his radar operator picked the raider up on his A.I set. The bomber was hit in a fusillade of 20mm

cannon shells and .303 rounds, plunging to earth at East Wittering, Sussex.

The press lauded Cunningham with the epithet 'Cats Eyes', it being suggested he had exceptional night vision. He hated the nickname, but to preserve the A.I radar secret Cunningham endured the pretence that it was all down to a diet of carrots. It was a silly tale, but it gained credibility with the public.

Of the reality, Cunningham's biographer, C F Rawnsley wrote:

"At last, after all the long months of trial and error, of strain and worry and

frustration, he [Cunningham] *had come to grips with the enemy. The good news was flashed immediately to Group HQ, to Fighter Command HQ and to the Air Ministry. There was solid wreckage on the ground to justify the faith of all those who had worked so hard for so long to bring the radar night fighter into its own."*

In terms of Britain's aerial night defence, a corner had been turned. The C-in-C, RAF Fighter Command, Air Marshal Sir Sholto Douglas, was heartened by the news. Of his predecessor, Air Chief Marshal Sir Hugh Dowding, his biographer noted:

"He was sorry to lose the chance of seeing to fruition his work on airborne radar and the like, especially as it had reached a very interesting stage."

INFLICTED HEAVY DAMAGE

By early 1941, Britain's night fighting capability was in a better place. In other areas, too, there were developments. Among them, radar guided AA guns and radar searchlights. Meanwhile, the Mosquito was under development and ultimately proved a potent night fighter. Nevertheless, even by the spring of 1941,

German raiders were statistically unlikely to encounter night fighters.

Generally, it is accepted that the Blitz ended on 11 May 1941, coinciding with the German assault on Russia. A consequence was that the Luftwaffe could no longer sustain concentrated air attacks on Britain, the Blitz finally petering out after eight months and five days.

Although the Blitz failed to bring about the collapse the Germans anticipated, it had not been unprofitable for them. Most rewarding was the adverse effect on aircraft production, seriously impaired by the destruction of factories and enforced

Above Although the Dornier 17-Z took heavy losses during daylight operations in 1940, the losses of all German bombers decreased once the Luftwaffe turned to mainly night attacks over Britain. Here, an officer of KG 2 supervises the loading of 50 kg bombs into his aircraft prior to a night raid. The pale blue undersides of the aircraft have been roughly painted over in black for night operations.
Left Sgt Pilot Harold Howes, a Hurricane pilot with 85 Squadron, was a successful day fighter 'ace' who was killed in a flying accident on a fruitless 'Fighter Night' operation during the Blitz after losing control and crashing east of London on the night of 22 December 1940.

dispersal of plant. The Germans also inflicted heavy damage on commercial and residential property for *relatively* insignificant losses in aircraft and crews.

In that respect, the RAF's night fighting capability across 1940 and 1941 did not significantly influence the outcomes of the Blitz either way. And neither did its existence greatly hamper the Luftwaffe's efforts, even when the RAF's night prowess was greatly improved. ■

The Lone Wolf

Most 'Cats' Eyes' sorties were unsuccessful, but one man became the highest scoring RAF pilot of the Blitz. With a hatred of the enemy and astonishing night vision, he was deemed 'too old' to be a fighter pilot but ended up becoming an outstanding hero.

On a moonlit night in September 1916, searchlights probed to find Zeppelin Schütte-Lanz II as it flew up the Thames Estuary. Meanwhile, brothers James and Richard Stevens were asleep in their cottage near Gravesend when their mother called:

'Boys, quick! He's coming down on fire!'

Rushing to the bedroom window, they cheered as the airship split into two angry red balls of fire and fell to earth north of the river.

What they had witnessed was the first successful night fighter interception in history over British soil, carried out by Lt William Leefe-Robinson, an event covered in the opening section of this publication.

In that moment, Richard decided what he wanted to be when he grew up: a night fighter pilot. It was an impossible and dream. And yet, 25 years later, he became just that: the RAF's greatest night fighter pilot of the Blitz stalking his prey in that very same patch of sky.

Growing up, Richard spent hours on nocturnal country walks, his siblings remembered him '...*at home in the dark - the night instincts of a cat!'*. He also became a crack shot. Firing an air pistol at 78rpm records suspended from washing lines, he delighted in getting pellets *through* the centre hole and was mortified if he missed and the discs shattered. But he rarely missed.

Already, he had excellent night vision and superb marksmanship.

TRAGIC ACCIDENT

In 1928, an adventurous spirit led him to go farming in Australia, but life became dull. He needed new adventures. Enlisting in the Palestine Police Force, he served for four years and felt affinity with both Jews and Arabs. Richard's great hero was now Lawrence of Arabia, with Lawrence's *'Seven Pillars of Wisdom'* becoming his 'Bible'.

By 1936, Richard was back in Britain, married to Mabel and learning to fly. Qualifying as a pilot, he flew airliners at Croydon wearing Arab head-dress in the cockpit, echoing his obsessive fascination with T E Lawrence. Eccentricity aside, an ability to see in the dark stood him in good stead on night flights between Croydon and Paris. A colleague recalled:

Facing Page Unlikely hero: Flight Lieutenant Richard Playne Stevens DSO DFC & Bar.

Right The second victim which fell to Richard Stevens' guns on the night of 15/16 January 1941 was this Heinkel 111 which he sent into the sea off Canvey Island.

Below Left This is the Heinkel 111 sent flaming into the ground at Wellesbourne on the night of 8 April 1941, pictured with two of the crew members shortly before its fateful last sortie. Seated on the fuselage is Feldwebel Hans Kaufhold who was alarmed to see Stevens closing in on his bomber through the night sky.

Middle Left The famous painting by Eric Kennington of Richard Stevens in the cockpit of his Hurricane prior to a night sortie. In the engagement with a Heinkel 111 on 8 April 1941, Hans Kaufhold on board the bomber said: 'There, quite clearly seen in the glare of our burning aircraft, a black helmeted figure was silhouetted in the open cockpit.'

Bottom Left This garish and dramatic piece of artwork was painted by Richard Stevens onto the engine cowling of his Hurricane, depicting a red devil spearing a swastika emblazoned eagle.

'If you wanted to find thick fog, you only had to go to Croydon. But Stevens' night sight was incredible. Not only could he see in the fog and mist, in the dark, but he had the instincts of a homing pigeon.'

As war loomed, Richard enlisted in the RAFVR but continued as an airline pilot. Then, with war declared, he flew army co-operation flights and 'target' aircraft training anti-aircraft gunners. But he wanted to get at the enemy. His advanced years, though, ruled him out as a fighter or bomber pilot. But Richard was not letting that get in the way of things.

Meanwhile, Mabel and the couple's children, twins John and Frances, were involved in a tragic accident.

In October 1940, a paraffin stove overturned causing a fire in which 21-month-old Frances died. Richard was devastated and became estranged from Mabel.

Later, it was reported his wife and children had been killed in the Blitz, a story which Richard did nothing to dispel and possibly encouraged. It is a tale which persisted across the years and is still widely repeated as one of the enduring myths of the Blitz.

FIGHTER PILOT

By late 1940, after relentlessly pestering, Richard was finall posted to train as a fighter pilot, but he was not expected to succeed.

Got Two Raiders In Night

THE R A F pilot who recently shot down two enemy night raiders in the London area in one night is Pilot Officer Richard Playne Stevens.

This was disclosed last night by the announcement that he has been awarded the D.F.C.

He chased each of the enemy machines for more than 100 miles in the darkness before destroying them at extremely short range.

In one instance he followed the raider almost to ground level from 30,000 feet (more than five miles up).

All Weathers

"He has shown the utmost keenness and determination for operations in all conditions of weather," says the official announcement.

Pilot-Officer Stevens was born at Tonbridge in 1909. Formerly a sergeant in the R A F, he was commissioned in the R A F V R last November. His wife lives at Ditchling, Sussex.

Above Right How Richard Stevens' first two victories were reported in the newspapers of the period. As time went on, Richard would garner many more column inches of press coverage with attendant adulation and hero worship.

His instructor recalled:

'We were used to dealing with young and inexperienced pilots. Onto this scene burst thirty-one-year-old Stevens – vastly more experienced than any of us instructors! He was an incredibly competent bad weather pilot, and we could have taught him to fly Hurricanes in a week. But the 'system' demanded he stay the full course. This contributed to his impatience - he regarded this time as interrupting his programme of getting to work against the Germans.'

His age, though, stood against him. Being a fighter pilot was a young man's game. Nevertheless, in November 1940, Richard was posted to 151 Squadron at RAF Wittering as a night-fighter pilot. Here, on the night of 15/16 January 1941, he found success for the first time - finely honed flying skills, remarkable night-vision and expert marksmanship all came together, seeing his nascence as an 'ace' during a 'Cats' Eyes' patrol.

First, over Essex, he found a Dornier 17, sending it flaming into the ground. There were no survivors.

Stevens, momentarily blacking out from excessive 'G' forces in a dive from 30,000ft, stressed his Hurricane to an extent it was grounded. Taking up another Hurricane that night, he found further prey, putting a Heinkel into the sea off Canvey Island.

Landing at Gravesend, Stevens strode into the crew hut to find exhausted pilots simply lounging around. Wing Commander Cosby recalled:

'Suddenly, in strode a chap wearing a sheepskin jacket and flying boots. Looking around, he demanded: 'Why aren't you lot airborne?' He was told in no uncertain words of one syllable, and a few expletives, what he could do.

'We asked him who the hell he was, where he came from, and in what? He told us from Wittering, in a Hurricane. We told him: 'Bloody well go back there!'

Above Left The last six victories claimed by Richard Stevens were secured over Junkers 88 bombers. This aircraft of Lehrgeschwader 1 has had its blue undersides painted matt black to make it less visible at night. However, such measures did not hinder Richard Stevens in picking out his quarry in the darkness of night.

Above The shattered wreckage of the Hurricane flown by Flt Lt Richard Stevens after he crashed for unknown reasons near Gilze Rijen in The Netherlands.

He said his name was Stevens. We'd never heard of him.'

They soon would.

CRASHING IN FLAMES

Richard's first 'kill' was immortalised by war artist Eric Kennington in 'Stevens Rocket', published with a Kennington portrait of Stevens himself in the *London Illustrated News*.

Admitted to hospital with a burst eardrum caused by diving from 30,000ft on that engagement, Richard wrote to his father:

'I resent congratulations for a job 9/10ths of the RAF could have done as easily or better. I have two Huns to my credit. Now they have added a DFC.'

His first 'kill' after recovery was a bomber seen against the moon's reflection on the sea. The raider stood no chance. Then, on 8 April, another victory sent a bomber crashing in flames near Wellesbourne. Two days later, Stevens flew through the exploding debris of a Heinkel, his score rising exponentially. And while most RAF fighter pilots struggled to even fly a Hurricane at night, let alone shoot anything down, Stevens excelled and revelled in it. His talent was extraordinary, his success prodigious.

One of his victims, a traumatised air gunner Feldwebel Hans Kaufhold of 3./KG 55, told his story:

'We were flying slowly at under one hundred feet in misty conditions. I thought we were invisible. Suddenly, I looked up and saw the shadow of a night fighter right on top of us. I just could not believe it as the cockpit and propeller slowly moved inside our tail plane. When he opened-up with his cannon, I thought he had collided with us because our debris was all over him. But there, quite clearly seen in the glare of our burning aircraft, a black helmeted figure was silhouetted in the open cockpit.'

COVERED IN BLOOD

In a short and meteoric career, Stevens became legendary and steadily racked up his score. Newspapers lauded him as 'Cats Eyes', a senior RAF officer describing him as the 'Lone Wolf'.

Once, when a bomber exploded in front of him, the bloody remains of an airman splattered across his Hurricane. He refused to let his mechanic wash it off:

'How he landed in the dark I don't know. The windscreen had a large hole in it. The

Above The Cuthbert Orde drawing of Flight Lieutenant Richard Stevens, DSO DFC & Bar.
Facing Page Below A hero at rest. The temporary grave marker for Richard Stevens in The Netherlands pictured just after the end of the war.

oil tank was punctured and dented, and we found hair and bits of bone stuck to the leading edge of the port wing. The tips of the propeller blades were covered in blood.'

Meanwhile, Stevens painted a colourful dragon onto his Hurricane, an RAF ensign wrapped in its tail as it speared a swastika emblazoned eagle.

Stevens developed dangerous tactics to track his quarry, deliberately flying into anti-aircraft barrages where the bombers would be, picking them off with consummate marksmanship. Often, his canopy would open for better visibility, but this sucked carbon monoxide exhaust fumes into the cockpit and temperatures plummeted to below zero.

One night, told the weather was too bad to fly, he was having none of it, taking off anyway. On another occasion, the airfield was bombed. Stevens was told he could not take off because the runway lights weren't on. Enraged, he shouted:
'I don't need bloody lights. I'll get the bastard!'

And he did.

'A HATRED OF THE HUN'

Stevens continued to claim victories, and at the end of June 1941 sent a Junkers 88 into the North Sea as victory number twelve. In July, he got number thirteen, keeping the enemy silhouetted against the distant Northern Lights before the North Sea eventually swallowed it up.

BLITZ GALLANTRY

As the most successful RAF night fighter pilot of the Blitz – despite all the odds being stacked against him – Richard Playne Stevens was decorated with the DSO as well as the DFC and Bar. The citations to those awards were published in the London Gazette and tell their own stories of extraordinary courage and extreme fortitude.

Distinguished Flying Cross

The London Gazette citation, published on 4 February 1941, for the award of DFC read as follows:
"This officer has performed outstanding work on night fighting operations during recent weeks. One night in January 1941, he shot down two hostile aircraft in the London area. In both these engagements he chased the enemy over 100 miles before destroying each at extremely short range. In one instance he followed the enemy aircraft almost to ground level from 30,000 feet. He has shown the utmost keenness and determination for operations in all conditions of weather."

Bar to Distinguished Flying Cross

The London Gazette citation, published on 29 April 1941, for a Bar to the DFC read as follows:
"This officer has done particularly outstanding work with his squadron on night operations and has on three occasions shot down two enemy aircraft in one night. Pilot Officer Stevens shows a great determination to attack the enemy and is prepared to fly under the most difficult weather conditions. His courage, determination, thoroughness and skill have set an excellent example to his unit."

Note: Both the DFC and the Bar to the DFC were awarded to Richard Playne Stevens by His Majesty King George VI in an investiture at Buckingham Palace on 20 May 1941.

Distinguished Service Order

The London Gazette citation, published on 12 December 1941, for the award of DSO read as follows:
"This officer has shown himself to be a fearless and outstanding night fighter pilot. One night in October 1941, flying at sea level, he intercepted a Junkers 88 off the East Anglian coast. The raider immediately turned and flew towards the continent at maximum speed, but Flight Lieutenant Stevens gave chase and slowly overhauled it. The raider then opened fire with his guns and began to drop his bombs singly. Columns of water were shot up as the result of the explosions, but Flight Lieutenant Stevens swerved round them and, closing into short range, shot down the enemy aircraft at almost sea level. He has destroyed at least 14 hostile aircraft at night."

By summer, night raids all but stopped, but Stevens was inevitably was sent over occupied Europe to seek out the enemy there. Group Captain Tom Gleave was Station Commander at RAF Manston:

'Night intruding was in its infancy and 'Steve' was the pioneer. He was someone I admired tremendously. Although quiet, and very much a loner, he was imbued with a hatred of the Hun.'

Eventually, in his all-black Hurricane, Stevens set out for Gilze-Rijen airfield in the Netherlands on 15 December 1941. Shooting down one Junkers 88, and damaging another, his Hurricane inexplicably crashed nearby, killing him instantly.

Tom Gleave:' The ops room said they heard 'Steve' calling but couldn't make out

what he was saying. Then, nothing more was heard from him. As the night ticked away, the sad truth dawned on us all.'

The bright star that had been Flt Lt Richard Stevens, DSO, DFC & Bar, had been snuffed out. The RAF's highest scoring night fighter pilot of the Blitz, he was the only one to achieve results without radar.

In a career of less than a year, he shot down 15 bombers, had half a claim over one and also two 'probables' and another 'damaged'.

When Stevens was killed, his fame all but died with him. Writing of Stevens, author H E Bates summed it up:

'He is dead now – you are the living. His was the sky – and yours is the earth because of him.' ∎

Attackers & Defenders

During air attacks against Britain between 1939 and 1945, both sides used a variety of aircraft types. For the night attacks particularly, many Luftwaffe and RAF aircraft were not specifically designed for the purpose to which they were ultimately put.

In the years prior to the Second World War, neither the Luftwaffe nor the RAF envisaged a scenario involving a sustained bombing campaign against the British Isles. Thus, Germany had not seen any need for heavy, long-range strategic bombers and the RAF had not anticipated any special need to develop a night fighter force. When the Blitz got underway in September 1940, both sides were faced with a degree of necessary improvisation.

For the defenders, use was initially made of aircraft like the Defiant and Blenheim, although the Beaufighter was just coming into service and proved useful to the RAF's night fighting capability.

The Spitfire and Hurricane were sometimes used on night interceptions, with the Hurricane used as a night fighter over Britain and an intruder over bomber bases on the continent to catch enemy aircraft landing or taking-off.

A later addition, the Mosquito, proved a highly effective night fighter – especially when fitted with Airborne Interception

radar and operating under ground-controlled interception.

THE OPPOSITION

On the Luftwaffe side, the same bomber aircraft used on daylight operations over Britain during 1939 and 1940 were now engaged on the night bombing sorties.

All of the main types, while tried and tested in combat, were only medium bombers and could only carry a moderate payload when compared to Allied strategic bombers However, these bombers did have the range to reach every part of the British Isles from their bases in occupied Europe.

With the introduction of the Dornier 217 came a very much 'upgraded' Dornier 17, although the type was not used over the British Isles in anything like the numbers necessary to make any difference to the air assault. This, of course, was a common thread running through all Luftwaffe bomber operations against Britain once the Blitz proper ended in May 1941.

Later additions to the bomber force

included the Messerschmitt 410; fast, but with a small bomb load, it was never destined to make any significant impact in the air campaign. Similarly, the Focke-Wulf 190 – designed as a fighter – made an appearance as a fighter-bomber carrying out day and night attacks against targets in the south and south-east.

By 1944 the Luftwaffe had introduced its only strategic bomber of the Second World War: the Heinkel 177 'Greif' (or Griffon). However, the type only ever came into service in small numbers and was plagued with engine problems.

There were, of course, other types employed by both sides during the air war over Britain. However, those detailed on the following pages represent the major types used during the Luftwaffe's air campaign against Britain, along with the RAF's defenders. ∎

Above The cannon armed Hurricane IIc was used on night fighter and intruder operations from 1941 but had limited usefulness because it was essentially a day fighter with no airborne radar.

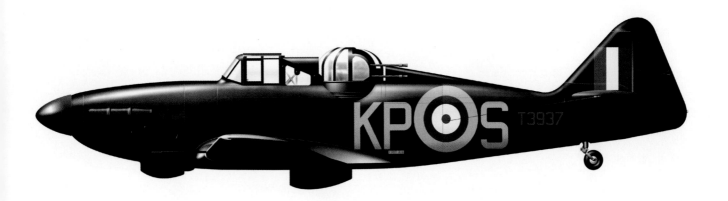

BOULTON PAUL DEFIANT MK I

The Defiant was of relatively conventional construction but its all-important turret singled it out as unusual for a single-engine fighter. It had been conceived as a 'bomber formation destroyer' at a time when the concept of fighter-escorted bombers attacking Britain had not been foreseen.

Whilst conventional wisdom might have us believe that this was a hopelessly outmoded design concept for modern air fighting, it was certainly not as ill-conceived as has often been suggested. Such suggestions inevitably arise from its poor performance during the daylight fighting of the Battle of Britain where it was improperly deployed and proved no match against enemy fighters and the tactics then employed by both sides.

Certainly, it lacked forward firing guns and had to be manoevred into a fighting position by its pilot in for the gunner to get a bead on his quarry. It was never designed for fighter-on-fighter combat and

its daylight participation in the air war over Britain thus had to be curtailed in the light of its poor performance against single-seat fighters.

However, there is no truth in the story that German fighter pilots, having fist mistaken them for Hurricanes, learned how to deal with the turreted fighters as a result.

From late 1940 onwards, the Defiant was utilised for night fighting operations - a role in which it achieved a degree of success. It thus became a useful weapon in RAF Fighter Command's early efforts to counter the Luftwaffe's night offensive.

Technical data:
- Dimensions: Span – 39ft 4in,
  Length – 35ft 4 in.
- Power Plant: Rolls Royce Merlin III,
  delivering 1,030 hp at 16,250 ft
- Maximum Speed: 304 mph
- Initial Rate of Climb: 2,120 ft per minute

Above The Defiant proved to be unsuitable for daylight operations and suffered heavy casualties during 1940.
Top Right The Boulton Paul Defiant was not a success as a day fighter during the Battle of Britain but went on to serve in a useful function as a night fighter.
Top Left The Fraser Nash type 'A' powered gun turret, fitted with four x Browning .303 machine guns, was the Defiant's armament. The canvas pouches were to collect the fired cartridge cases.

Top The Blenheim Mk IF carried a ventral gun pack comprising four Browning .303 machine guns which can be seen here under the fuselage.
Above The Blenheim production line at the Bristol Aeroplane Company, 1939.
Left The Blenheim also carried a defensive mid-upper gun turret equipped with a single Vickers .303 'K' Gun.

BRISTOL BLENHEIM MK I F

Between 1934 and the spring of 1935, the Bristol Aeroplane Company Ltd built a fast civil transport aircraft of advanced design to the order of Lord Rothermere in his capacity as a private customer. When this proved faster than most contemporary military aircraft, Lord Rothermere presented the aircraft to the nation.

From Rothermere's aircraft, the manufacturers developed the Blenheim Mk I bomber, of which the prototype first flew in June 1936. At the request of the Air Ministry, the Bristol Aeroplane Company also developed a fighter

version, the Blenheim Mk If. During the Battle of Britain, the Blenheim Mk If was used as both a day and night fighter. As a day fighter it had limited value unless used against unescorted bombers, although by 1940 it was unable to catch the German bombers then in use if engaged in a tail-chase. The Blenheim could not be pitched against escorted raids of the nature being experienced, for example, in the 11 Group area at the height of the battle and was clearly no match when pitted against either the Messerschmitt 109 or Messerschmitt 110.

As a night fighter, however, it achieved some early successes in the RAF's nocturnal operations against enemy bombers.

Technical Data
- Dimensions: Span 56 ft 4 in, Length 39 ft 9 in
- Power Plant: Two x Bristol Mercury VIII engines, each delivering 840 hp
- Maximum Speed: 260 mph
- Initial Rate of Climb: 1,540 ft per minute
- Service Ceiling: 27,280 ft
- Armament: Turreted Vickers .303 'K' gun plus

BRISTOL BEAUFIGHTER I

Like the Blenheim, the Beaufighter started out as a private-venture design as a twin-engine, cannon armed fighter. By July 1938, however, the Air Ministry decided to adopt the type and it immediately went into production. By the end of 1940 only 110 had been built.

The aircraft entered service in August 1940, and although originally intended as a day fighter it quickly became apparent it was more suited to the night fighter role, largely because of ample space in which to fit Airborne Interception (AI) radar. Like other cannon-equipped RAF aircraft that were put in service around this time, the weapon proved troublesome with feed mechanism issues. Also, vibration in the mountings causing inaccurate firing. Once these problems were ironed out, the Beaufighter became an impressive night-fighter.

Although it was only just coming on stream with a few Fighter Command squadrons and units as the Battle of Britain drew towards its zenith, no successful engagements had taken place by the end of September. However, when employed exclusively in the night-fighting role during late 1940 and 1941 it achieved notable successes against Luftwaffe bombers.

Technical Data
- Dimensions: Span 57 ft 10 in, Length 41 ft 8 in
- Power Plants: Two x Bristol Hercules III
- Maximum Speed: 320 mph
- Initial Rate of Climb: 1,600 ft per minute
- Service Ceiling: 19,000 ft
- Armament: Four x 20 mm Hispano cannon

Top Right The Bristol Beaufighter was a powerfully potent night fighter, fitted with a battery of four x 20 mm Hispano cannon under the nose and six x Browning .303 machine guns in the wings. In this photograph, the dull black finish for night operations can be seen along with the various aerials for the Airborne Interception radar.
Right The spacious Beaufighter cockpit. The gunsight is directy ahead of the pilot, the gun button on top right of control column yoke.

Above By the end of 1940, only a relatively small number of Beaufighters had been built by the Bristol Aeroplane Company. The type went on to become a useful and effective night fighter during the Blitz. Powerfully armed, and equipped with Airborne Interception radar, the aircraft achieved a good success rate.

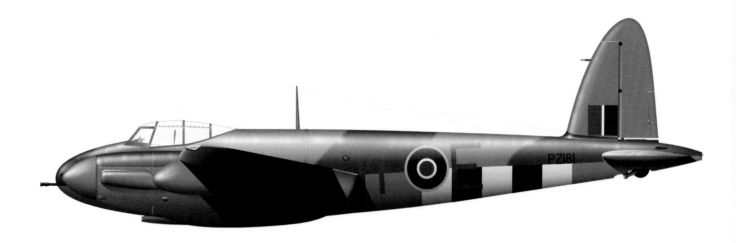

DE HAVILLAND MOSQUITO NF MK II

The de Havilland Mosquito was a twin-engine multirole combat aircraft, unusual in that its frame was constructed mostly of wood, it was nicknamed the 'Mossie' or 'Wooden Wonder'. In 1941, it was one of the fastest operational aircraft in the world.

Originally conceived as an unarmed fast bomber, the Mosquito's use evolved during the war into many roles, including low- to medium-altitude daytime tactical bomber, high-altitude night bomber, pathfinder, day or night fighter, fighter-bomber, intruder, maritime strike, and photo-reconnaissance aircraft.

Conceived as a bomber in 1936, it first flew in November 1940. By then, the Air Ministry had also decided to develop the aircraft as a fighter. Ultimately, it became one of the most successful of all RAF night fighter aircraft, first coming into operational service in 1942.

As it was developed throughout the war, different versions of the night fighter were built and equipped with Airborne Interception radar.

The aircraft carried a powerful nose armament of cannon and machine guns, enabling it to pack a mightily powerful punch. It carried a crew of two.

Technical Data
- Dimensions: Span 54 ft 2 in, Length 41 ft 2 in
- Power Plants: Two x Rolls Royce Merlin 21 or 23 engines
- Maximum Speed: 370 mph
- Service Ceiling: 28,000 ft
- Range: 1,400 miles
- Armament: Four x 20mm Hispano cannon and 4 x .303 Browning machine guns

Right The potent punch! An armourer loads belted ammunition into the four nose-mounted Browning .303 machine guns of a Mosquito. Beneath the nose can be seen the apertures for the four 20 mm cannon.

Top A dramatic image showing a night fighter Mosquito test firing its four Browning .303 machine guns and four 20 mm cannon at the butts. The destructive punch delivered by this battery of weaponry is powerfully demonstrated in this photograph.
Above The famous de Havilland Mosquito was used in a wide range of roles, including as a night fighter. Fast, heavily armed and with airborne interception radar, it was a very successful fighter when pitted against night raiders

HAWKER HURRICANE IIC

The Hurricane low-wing monoplane single seat fighter was designed by Sydney Camm and developed by Hawker Aircraft Ltd. as a private venture. The prototype first flew on 6 November 1935 and the Hurricane came into front-line service with the RAF in January 1938. It became the most numerous fighter aircraft in RAF service during the Battle of Britain.

The airframe was extremely rugged and could take considerable punishment, due in part to its fabric, wood and tubular steel rear fuselage construction and a sturdy airframe centre-section. Its wide undercarriage was also a useful attribute when landing.

Following the Battle of Britain, and through the Blitz of 1941, the Hurricane I was the principal single-seat night fighter in Fighter Command. Then, by 1942 the cannon-armed Mk IIc had come into service – its four x 20mm cannon replacing the earlier armament of eight x .303 machine guns and with the Rolls Royce Merlin XX replacing the earlier Merlin III.

The aircraft also performed as a night intruder over occupied Europe but was withdrawn in 1943.

Technical Data
- Dimensions: Span 40 ft, Length 32 ft 3 in
- Power Plant: Rolls-Royce Merlin XX
- Max Speed: 340 mph
- Service Ceiling: 36,000 ft
- Range: 600 miles
- Armament: Four x 20mm Hispano cannon

Top Right Having given valuable service as a day fighter during the Battle of France and Britain with eight x .303 Browning machine guns, the Hurricane I was ultimately upgraded to the Hurricane II with four x 20 mm Hispano cannon – a game-changer in terms of hitting power. With four cannon, the Hurricane was a moderate success at night.
Right The cockpit of a Hurricane IIc.

Below An armourer feeds belts of 20 mm ammunition into the gun bays of a Hurricane IIc night fighter. This armament of four 20 mm cannon gave a much greater destructive power than the eight .303 Browning machine guns with which the earlier Hurricanes were equipped.
Bottom A comparison photograph showing the relative sizes of the 20 mm cannon round (left) against the rifle calibre .303 Browning ammunition, the latter being used on earlier Hurricanes.

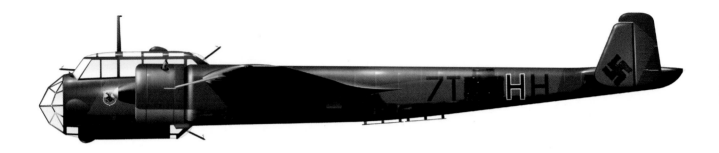

DORNIER 17 Z-2

The Dornier 17 high-wing monoplane was intended by Dornier-Werke G.m.b.H as a commercial aircraft, but a demonstration of the prototype in the autumn of 1934 brought no orders from Lufthansa. A bomber version first flew in 1935 and was developed for the Luftwaffe and went on to achieve some success in the Spanish Civil War.

Eight variants of the Dornier 17, in addition to two variants of a type known as the Dornier 215, were used in 1940 as bombers or reconnaissance aircraft. The bomber version of the Dornier 17 were types in the 'Z' series, with the reconnaissance version being the 'P'. The slim fuselage of the Dornier 17 earned it the nickname 'Flying Pencil'.

The type, as a bomber, served on through the Blitz into 1941, but was then otherwise pretty much phased-out of front-line operational service. It carried a crew of four.

Technical Data (Dornier 17 Z-2)
- Dimensions: Span 59 ft, length 53 ft 5.5 in
- Power Plants: Two x Bramo-Fafnir 323 P radial engines, each delivering 1,000 hp
- Maximum Speed: 265 mph with normal load
- Service Ceiling: 26,740 ft
- Range: Normal, 745 miles (with overload tank 1,860 miles)
- Bomb Load: Normal, 2,200 lb (with maximum fuel, 1,100 lb)

Top Right A Dornier 17-Z pilot points out the emblem of his unit, 2/KG76, depicting a broken Union Jack shield, a toppling crown and a lion being struck by a bomb marked 'Made in Germany'. Although a mainstay of the Battle of Britain and earlys days of the Blitz, the Dornier 17 suffered significant losses.

Right This view through the nose glazing of a Dornier 17-Z showing a formation fanned out in front. Massed daylight attacks on Britain during September 1940 would have looked very much like this. Such formations allowed for greater and cohesive protection from fighter attack from the massed defensive guns carried by the bombers.

DORNIER 217 E-2

The Dornier 217 was classified as a heavy bomber and ordered by the Luftwaffe as early as 1937. However, the design, development and production process did not result in the type becoming operational until the latter half of 1941. Its initial deployment was with units operating against the British Isles and shipping in its coastal waters.

Several variants of the type eventually saw service on various battle fronts, although it was never produced in sufficient numbers or employed in a manner which had much impact on the scale or efficacy of German attacks on Britain. That said, it did participate in many devastating and disruptive attacks – including daylight 'Pirate' raids on Britain in 1942 and 1943.

Initial attempts to develop the aircraft as a dive-bomber were ultimately abandoned although night fighter versions were built and the Dornier 217 K-2 with an extended wingspan was developed to deliver the 'Fritz X' stand-off anti shipping missile.

The aircraft carried a crew of four.

Technical Data
- Dimensions: Span 62 ft 4 in, Length 59 ft 8.5 in
- Power Plants: Two x BMW 801-ML
- Maximum Speed: 273 mph
- Initial Rate of Climb: 710 ft per minute (with maximum internal bomb load)
- Service Ceiling: 24,600 ft (with maximum internal bomb load)
- Bomb Load: 8,818 lb

Top Right The Dornier 217 came into Luftwaffe service in 1941 and was used in daylight and night-time attacks on Britain. The aircraft shown here was captured and evaluated by the RAF at the end of the war but was later scrapped. Unfortunately, no examples of this aircraft type survive today.
Right The upper turret on a Dornier 217, fitted with a 13mm MG 131 gun.

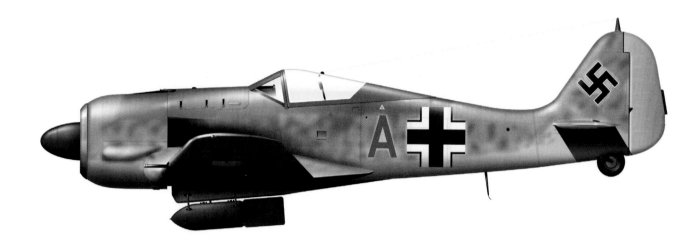

FOCKE-WULF 190 A-3

As a type, the Focke-Wulf 190 was initially designed and intended for use as a single-seat fighter aircraft and came into service with the Luftwaffe in that role from the autumn on 1941 where it proved a formidable opponent when pitted against the RAF's Spitfire V fighters which it seriously outclassed.

A number of models and variants of the Focke-Wulf 190 were built and put into service, but from 1942 the type was increasingly employed in the fighter-bomber role against targets in London and south east and, in particular, along the south and east coasts. (Note: For the purposes of this text we have taken the Focke-Wulf 190 A-3 as our example)

Usually carrying a single 500 kg bomb under the fuselage, the aircraft conducted devastating fast and low-level 'tip-and-run' raids against British towns, often shooting up the targets with cannon and machine gun fire to maximise the 'nuisance' effect and suppress light anti-aircraft fire.

Technical Data
• Dimensions: Span, 34 ft 5 in,
  Length 28 ft 10.5 in
• Power Plant: BMW 801 D-2
• Max Speed: 330 mph
• Initial Rate of Climb: 2,830 ft min
• Service Ceiling: 34,775 ft
• Range: 497 miles
• Armament: Two x 7.92mm MG17,
  two x 20mm MG151 cannon and
  two x 20mm MGFF cannon plus
  one underslung 250kg or 500kg bomb

Above The Focke-Wulf 190 was initially conceived as a fighter, and as shown in this image depicting the first intact aircraft of this type to fall into RAF hands on 23 June 1942. The Focke-Wulf 190 was later used in the fighter-bomber role conducting damaging 'Tip-and-Run' attacks against Britain.
Right The well laid-out cockpit of the Focke-Wulf also allowed excellent all-round visibility for the pilot.

Right The powerful BMW 801 engine of the Focke-Wulf 190 is shown in this view of the un-cowled power plant on the same captured example of the aircraft. The extreme front of the cowling comprised an armoured ring to offer protection against fire directed from ahead of the aircraft.

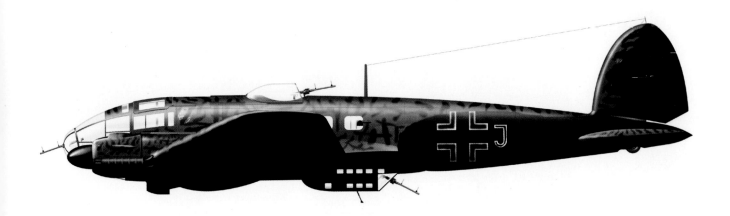

HEINKEL 111 H-3

The He 111 was a low-wing twin engine monoplane long-range bomber with a crew of four. It was developed by Ernst Heinkel Flugzeugwerke G.m.b.H and first flew in 1935 before entering service with the expanding Luftwaffe in 1937. Early models of the type took part in the Spanish Civil War and it became one of the mainstay bombers across all Luftwaffe air fleets during 1940. Nine different variants were used during 1940, including a version that operated with the Daimler-Benz DB 601 engine.

The aircraft proved too slow and too lightly armed to escape heavy losses during daylight action although became a successful night bomber. For simplicity, the technical data (below) selects just one of the models commonly in use, the He 111 H-3.

Technical Data
- Dimensions: Span 74 ft 3 in, length 54 ft 6 in
- Power Plants: Two x Junkers Jumo 211 D-1 engines, each delivering 1,200 hp
- Maximum Speed: 255 mph with normal load
- Service Ceiling: 25,500 ft
- Range: Normal – 1,540 miles; with additional fuel, 2,640 miles
- Bomb Load: Maximum 4,400 lb (with increased fuel load 2,134 lb)

Right A mainstay of the Luftwaffe's bomber arm during the Battle of Britain, and then the Blitz and beyond, the Heinkel 111 in its various types was popular with its crews but it suffered significant daylight losses. Night operations resulted in fewer losses, but a large number were still lost on operations or in accidents. Here, a Heinkel 111 which was damaged during a sortie over Britain has managed to make it back to its airfield in France, the aircrew safe but the aircraft wrecked.

Above Left In common with most Luftwaffe bomber types the Heinkel 111 had an extensively glazed nose section as evidence in this photograph taken during German pre-war exercises. Early versions of the aircraft had also been used in the Spanish Civil War, but it went on to become one of the Luftwaffe's principal bombers during the Blitz of 1940-41.
Above Right The Heinkel 111 had a number of defensive stations armed with 7.92mm MG 15 machine guns. This view shows a waist gunner at his position, with another gunner in the ventral gondola. At night, the gunners had the unenviable job of trying to spot near invisible stalking night fighters.

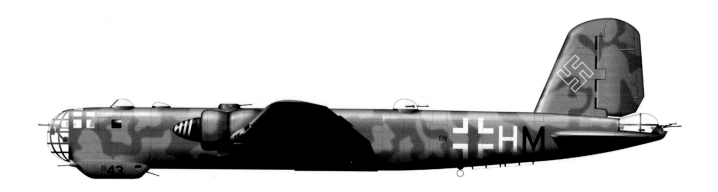

HEINKEL 117 A-5 'GREIF'

The Heinkel 177 'Greif' (Griffon) was intended to provide the Luftwaffe with a bomber aircraft which would allow it to conduct a major strategic bomber offensive. Unfortunately, type was beset with technical difficulties which were never fully resolved, its operational use being something of a disaster and beset by frequent engine fires. Had these issues been resolved, however, and had the aircraft been built and deployed in sufficient numbers then its impact during attacks on the British Isles might have been significant.

Conceived as early as 1937, it did not come into operational service until 1942 but only in relatively small numbers.

Its use against the British Isles really only began in 1944 when it was used with limited success during the so-called 'Little Blitz', or Operation Steinbock. However, its failings and shortcomings aside, the aircraft showed what it could do. With a maximum bomb load, the aircraft could climb to 23,000 over home territory and approach targets like London in a shallow dive where it could pick up a speed of 430 mph and evade night fighters and flak. For the Luftwaffe, though, it was too little too late – and with a flawed and problematic aircraft.

The aircraft carried a crew of six.

Technical Data
- Dimensions: Span, 103 ft 2 in, Length 72 ft 2 in
- Power Plants: Two x DB 610 24 x cylinder engines
- Max Speed: 351 mph (NB: see above)
- Initial Rate of Climb: 623 ft min
- Service Ceiling: 26,250 ft
- Range: 960 miles
- Bomb Load: Up to 15,000 lb

Above Coming into service too late to make any appreciable impact on Luftwaffe operations, a number of these large aircraft were shot down over the British Isles although it was not until the war had ended that the Allies finally got their hands on intact examples. This specimen was captured and test flown for evaluation purposes by the RAF.

Left The massive double undercarriage is shown to good effect in this photograph.

Right The Heinkel 177 'Greif', the Luftwaffe's only strategic bomber, came to attack on Britain late in the war, in small numbers and with limited success. The aircraft itself was also dogged with technical problems.

JUNKERS 88 A-1

The Junkers 88 low-wing monoplane first flew in December 1936 with the manufacturers, Junkers Flugzeug und Moterenwerke A.G intending it as a high-performance bomber with a turn of speed that would enable it to dispense with any fighter escort. Hopes of outdistancing any pursuing fighters were dashed, however, with the advent of the Spitfire and Hurricane. However, it remained a fast and agile aircraft and was considered the hardest of the German bombers to catch and shoot down.

Two variants, the A-1 and A-5, were used in 1940 but a wider range of variants were used in air operations against Britain from 1941 onwards. The aircraft carried a crew of four.

Technical Data (Junkers 88 A-1)
- Dimensions: Span, 59 ft 10.75 in increased in the A-5 to 65 ft 10.5 in) length, 47 ft 1 in
- Power Plants: Two x Junkers Jumo 211 B-1 engines, each delivering 1,200 hp
- Maximum Speed: 286 mph
- Service Ceiling: 26,500 ft
- Range: Normal, 1,553 miles
- Bomb Load: Normal, 3,968 lb; Maximum 5,510 lb

Above A Junkers 88 is refuelled and prepared for a nocturnal sortie against Britain. Again, the black under surfaces have been applied for night operations.

Above The Junkers 88 was also produced as a night fighter and was a dangerous threat to RAF aircraft over Britain, particularly bombers returning to their bases in East Anglia.
Left It was as a bomber, however, that the Junkers 88 was mostly engaged over Britain, with different versions of the type being used until the end of the war.

MESSERSCHMITT 410 A-1

The aircraft was essentially a development of its less than successful predecessor, the Messerschmitt 210, and was used extensively in night operations against the British Isles from mid-1943.

Designed as a Kampfzerstörer (Bomber-Destroyer), the type was intended as a fast light bomber or else could be engaged in the fighter role, in which it was primarily used in defence of the Reich. Against the Britain, though, it was used at night as a Schnellbomber, or fast bomber. Sleek and fast, the type could sometimes outrun even the RAF's Mosquito night fighters. A unique feature were two defensive and remotely operated rearward firing MG 131 13mm guns in barbettes on either side of the fuselage.

As with many Luftwaffe types operated later in the war, the numbers built and used ultimately had little significant impact in the conduct of the air campaign against Britain. It was, though, considered a generally excellent aircraft and had a noteworthy and high performance.

Technical Data
- Dimensions: Span, 53 ft 8 in, Length 40 ft 11.5 in
- Power Plants: Two x DB 603 A engines
- Max Speed: 388 mph
- Service Ceiling: 33,000 ft
- Range: 750 miles
- Bomb Load: Up to 2,200 lb

NOTE: Various sub-types of the aircraft depicted were used by both the attackers and defenders. Sometimes, the leading specifications for these sub-types varied in terms of performance, dimensions, engines, bomb loads etc. However, for illustrative purposes, the main variants are shown here.

Left This Messerschmitt 410 A-1/U2 was captured by the RAF in 1945 and is today preserved in the UK as part of the RAF Museum collection.

Above The unusual and remotely controlled rotating twin barbettes, each with a MG 131 13 mm machine gun, were a feature on of the Messerschmitt 410's fuselage.

JUNKERS 87

The Junkers 87 Stuka dive bomber was used in the early stages of the Battle of Britain against coastal targets, airfields and radar stations in the south of England. An effective weapon, it nevertheless lacked speed and range and required close fighter protection if it were to survive contact with RAF Spitfires and Hurricanes.

After 18 August 1940, it saw no further operational use over Britain until it resumed attacks against shipping in the English Channel in November 1940 – a role it continued until early 1941. Briefly, there was even a rather pointless involvement in a few night bombing raids against British targets. With a crew of two, the aircraft could carry a bomb load of up to 500 kg.

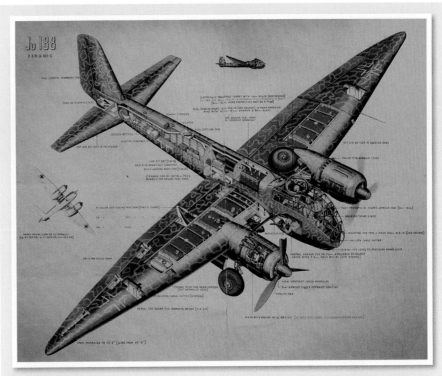

JUNKERS 188

Essentially this was a stop-gap development of the Ju88, the Junkers Ju188 was a four-seat medium bomber which featured a redesigned nose, longer wings with pointed tips, a new tail unit and a streamlined dorsal gun turret. These modifications made it more manoeuvrable than its predecessor and enhanced its high-altitude performance.

The type first flew in the spring of 1942, but despite being a useful aircraft, only 1,076 were completed before production ended at the beginning of 1944. Withdrawn as a bomber by the autumn of that year, it continued to serve in a reconnaissance role until the end of the war.

JUNKERS 86-P

One of the more unusual aircraft types operated by the Luftwaffe over Britain, the Junkers 86-P, was a high-altitude reconnaissance aircraft which conducted numerous photographic sorties over the mainland – usually only visible from the tell-tale vapour trail it left behind it. The aircraft conducted valuable post-strike reconnaissance over targets hit by the Luftwaffe during the Battle of Britain and later.

First tested in January 1940, the aircraft had a pressurised cabin, carried a crew of two and was fitted with turbocharged two-stroke opposed piston Diesel engines (the Junkers Jumo 207 A-1) and was able fly at altitudes of around 39,000 feet or higher, thus safely out of reach of RAF fighters.

FOCKE-WULF 200 'CONDOR'

Originally conceived as a four-engine airliner, the Focke-Wulf 200 'Condor' carried a crew of five and was operated by the Luftwaffe principally as a maritime patrol aircraft, carrying out valuable service in the Atlantic and Western Approaches as a commerce raider and conducting armed reconnaissance - although it did not operate over the British mainland.

Having a range of 3,560 km, the aircraft could carry up to 1,000 kg of bombs internally or 5,400 kg on external racks. The 'Condor' also had an endurance of 14 hours, its range and endurance meaning it could be successfully employed reporting on convoys for targeting by U-boats and leading to Winston Churchill calling the aircraft '...the scourge of the Atlantic.'

Sinking the Empress

Whilst the aerial Blitz against Britain was largely directed at land targets, the Luftwaffe also conducted a significant campaign against maritime assets on the high seas and around Britain's coastline.

The war at sea is largely thought of as being fought between surface vessels and submarines, and although this was very largely the case it was also a fact that air power played a large part in the conduct of German maritime operations. This was against dock installations, Royal Navy vessels and mercantile marine shipping plying commercial routes - the latter comprising transatlantic supply convoys and coastal shipping around the UK. Apart from the obvious military value of naval vessels, commercial shipping was transporting vital cargoes of military equipment and munitions, fuel and food. Thus, the disruption of this trade to a

seafaring island nation was an important strategic objective for Germany.

In respect of coastal convoys, these were almost routinely targeted by Luftwaffe aircraft. Indeed, the early stages of the Battle of Britain, during July and August 1940, saw a phase where heavy air attacks were launched against this coastal shipping. Meanwhile, Royal Navy dockyards such as the port facilities at Portland in Dorset, were also singled out for attention. Similarly, commercial docks at (among others) Liverpool, Southampton, Bristol, Glasgow and the Port of London were all bombed heavily when the Blitz got underway from 7 September 1940.

As to the Atlantic routes, the main threat came from the U-boat menace, although the Luftwaffe played its own important part in interrupting this trade with long-range aircraft. That role fell very largely to the four-engine Focke-Wulf 200 Condor maritime patrol bombers of Kampfgeschwader 40, mainly operating from bases in the west of France. Not only was the aircraft a potent and dangerous bomber which could engage and sink shipping, but it was also able to report back on the position of convoys to aid U-boat interceptions.

One of the Condor's major successes, though, was its role during October 1940 in the sinking of the RMS *Empress of*

Britain – at the time weighing in at 42,348 Gross Registered Tons, she was Britain's second largest ship and the tenth largest merchant vessel in the world. Its sinking would also be a major propaganda coup for Germany.

Construction of the *Empress* began at John Brown and Co, Clydebank, in November 1928 and she was launched in June 1930 by HRH The Prince of Wales, eventually leaving Southampton for Quebec on her maiden voyage on 27 May 1931, then under the flag of the Canadian Pacific Steamship Company. Plying her trade as a passenger liner, the *Empress of Britain* was ultimately requisitioned as a troop ship in September 1939. Completing several trooping passages across the first ten months or so of the war, she was on a journey from Cape Town to the UK in October 1940 with 205 military and civilian passengers and 416 crew under the captaincy of Captain Charles H Sapsworth.

However, it was while on that journey, and at 09.10 hrs on 26 October 1940, about 87 miles west of the Isle of Aran, when disaster struck.

A DIRECT HIT

At 04.07 hrs German time (03.07 hrs UK time) on 26 October 1940, a Condor of I./KG 40 lifted-off from Bordeaux-Mérignac, south-western France, to carry out an armed reconnaissance and weather forecasting flight north-west of Ireland. In command of the five-man crew was Oberleutnant Bernhard Jope. His mission that day would see him coming to the attention of not only the German public but also becoming a personality of interest to British military authorities.

Oberleutnant Jope's Condor flew north-north-west via Ireland and crossed the neutral southern Irish coast as dawn was breaking at about 08.30 hrs before flying along the west coast of Ireland, north to Erris Head at the north-western tip of

Above The emblem of KG 40 is seen here on one of its Condor aircraft. The ringed globe symbolised the long-range capabilities of the aircraft which was originally conceived as an airliner.

Above Right Listing and on fire, this was one of the last images of the Empress of Britain.

Right Crippled and in tow, the Empress of Britain was now being shadowed by a U-boat which ultimately delivered the coup de grace.

Far Right The official report photographs showing Jope's attack on the Empress of Britain.

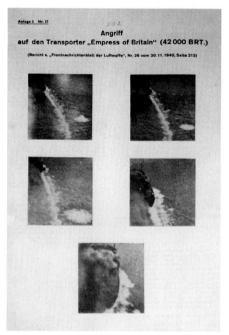

Ireland. From there, course was taken out across the sea. Jope then recorded the following:

'At 1010 hrs, after about half an hour flying time, a very large ship appeared to port. This was discovered very late due to bad visibility, cloud cover and rainy weather conditions. I was flying at about 800 meters and recognised a huge ship with three funnels which was heading for Northern Ireland at high speed.

'I changed course immediately, ordered my crew to action stations and flew around the ship in a wide turn to attack from behind in low level flight.

'During the attack, fire was opened with our cannon at about 400 metres.

'I approached from a height of 600 metres, went down to 200 metres and dropped a 250 kg bomb which struck the port side aft and caused a fire which quickly spread.'

Onboard the *Empress*, a correspondent for *The Times* recorded that the Condor first machine gunned the ship and then returned to drop a high explosive bomb which scored a direct hit. A third attack then set the liner ablaze.

Bernhard Jope continued his own account thus:

'Before and after the attack, there was defensive fire from machine guns as well as 2 cm and 4 cm guns and the bomb sight of our aircraft was destroyed on the first attack approach.

'The ship had already transmitted SOS calls that were intercepted by us.

'Immediately after the first run, and after another wide turn, a second stern attack was flown against the ship which was still steaming at a fairly high speed. The defensive fire in the second attack became even stronger. Due to the destroyed bomb sight the second bomb missed.

'I decided now, after the fire had already taken on considerable proportions, to fly head-on attacks so as not to be so heavily exposed to the rear defences. The ship made considerable evasive movements and steered a turn of 360° which made approach difficult. Two more head-on attacks were made and another bomb hit the target on the starboard foredeck. The defence fell almost completely silent during the last attack. The cloud of smoke was still increasing. The ship showed a slight list, and the entire hull was burning when our aircraft left. Our aircraft was hit by machine gun fire.'

'ABANDON SHIP'

Jope had dropped a total of six x 250 kg bombs, two of which hit the ship. He then reported the results of his attack by radio, under-estimating the ship at only 20,000-25,000 tons.

Jope then resumed the weather reconnaissance mission but had to head for Brest due to failure of the right outer engine which seized, the result of damage from gunfire from the *Empress*. However, Jope landed safely despite having flown on three engines for about an hour.

What happened on board the *Empress* is best illustrated by Steward James Donovan:

'About 40 or 50 passengers lay on the deck when the bombs began to fall. The stench left by the bombs was terrible. The Captain manoeuvred the liner so that the forward part was clear of smoke and flames.

'Some 300 people including women and children had gathered. The fire spread so quickly that the boats had to be got away with only four men in them so that they could be safely floated and afterwards pick up the passengers and crew.'

Right The four engines of the Focke-Wulf Condor helped give the aircraft its long-range capability, with the loss of one engine not necessarily impairing its ability to continue with a flight – as Jope discovered on 26 October 1940.
Below Right A Luftwaffe maritime map showing the sea area north of Ireland where the Empress of Britain was finally sent to the bottom.

Because of the fire, at 09.50 hrs Captain Sapsworth gave the order to abandon ship but leaving a skeleton crew on board. The survivors were rescued by HMS *Echo*, the anti-submarine trawler HMS *Cape Arcona* and Polish destroyer *Burza* which also took *Empress* in tow. However, this was not the end of the story.

Bernhard Jope reported the ship he had attacked was still afloat and this information was passed to the *Kriegsmarine* who sent a U-boat to investigate. The task was given to U-32, a type VIIA U-boat, which set sail from Lorient on 24 October 1940 on what would be its ninth war patrol. In command was 27-year-old Oberleutnant zur See Hans Jenisch who was on his sixth war patrol since taking command of U-32 in February 1940.

As Jenisch was headed towards the last known position of the *Empress of Britain*, HMS *Marauder* and HMS *Thames* had taken over towing duties, assisted by the tugs HMS *Seaman* and *Raider*. They were escorted by HMS *Broke* and HMS *Sardonyx*, as well as RAF Sunderland flying boats which flew overhead during daylight. All were unaware that they were being stalked by the U-32 for nearly 24 hours.

Finally, Jenisch got into position to fire two torpedoes, of which the second one he fired hit and caused a massive explosion which the ships accompanying thought was due to fire reaching her fuel tanks. Only when the Germans released a communiqué saying it was sunk by a U-boat did the truth become known. Jenisch then fired a third torpedo and *Empress* began to fill with water and list heavily. With the tugs releasing the tow ropes at 02.05 hrs on 28 October 1940, the *Empress of Britain* slipped beneath the waves north-west of Bloody Foreland, County Donegal, where she still lies upside down on the seabed.

British records show that 45 passengers and crew lost their lives between the air attack on 26 October and *Empress* sinking on 28 October 1940.

From a German perspective, the sinking of the *Empress of Britain* was a massive propaganda coup. Jope was awarded

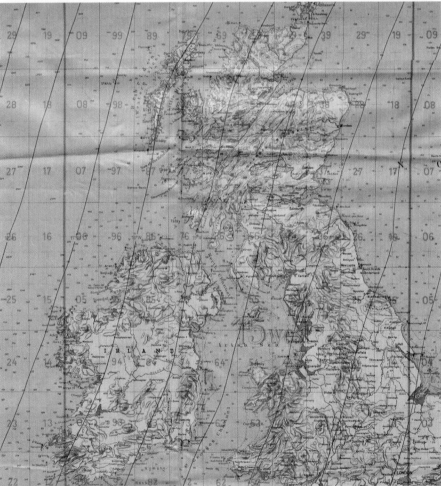

the Ritterkreuz (Knight's Cross) on 30 December 1940, Jenisch already having received the award on 7 October 1940.

The loss of the *Empress of Britain* was a severe blow to British trooping capabilities, but its sinking also demonstrated that the Luftwaffe was able to exercise its air power to good effect, and not only against British targets on the mainland but far out to sea, too.

The Blitz was not simply confined to towns and cities. British assets were in danger wherever they were in range of German bombers. ■

The Luftwaffe's 'Marie Celeste'

The loss of Luftwaffe aircraft over Britain during the period of the Blitz was by no means an unusual event. However, the arrival of one German bomber left the authorities puzzled.

During the early hours of 28 November 1940, with the Blitz in full swing, a Junkers 88 A-5 made what might be called an uncontrolled descent into the terrain at Blindley Heath in Surrey. The aircraft was a machine belonging to 6/ KG 77, 3Z+EP, Werk Nummer 7116, and it had struck power cables at around 01.35 hrs before crashing nearby and breaking into several large sections. Locals reported seeing parachutes just before the crash, but as things transpired this can only have been a figment of their imagination. Nevertheless, a manhunt was initiated for what were supposedly four Luftwaffe airmen who were clearly at large somewhere in the Surrey countryside after investigators examined the wreckage in the light of dawn found no trace of casualties in the remains of the cockpit. The search for survivors, however, was subsequently widened when no trace of the men could be found locally. It turned out to be a fruitless search.

Meanwhile, somewhere near Reims in France, four rather shaken Luftwaffe fliers were doubtless settling down to restorative coffees or Cognac, all of them completely unaware that a huge hunt was going on for them on the other side of the English Channel! The hunt, however, was not given any let with the discovery of items in the cockpit that surely indicated the crew must be hiding up somewhere locally or else 'on the run'.

Rummaging amongst the strewn and scattered documents, RAF intelligence officers found a notebook which had some hastily scribbled sentences written on its cover. Translated, the text read:

'I must have a DF (direction finding) bearing.'

Then, on another page, the message: *'Pass around. Bale out'.*

But exactly what had gone wrong on 3Z+EP's final flight is difficult to establish precisely.

Since 3/KG 77 do not seem to have been rostered for any sorties over Britain that night, then it may have simply been the case that the crew became lost on an internal flight over Occupied Europe.

Certainly, bad weather and poor visibility, including fog, had been a problem over parts of the continent that night and may have been a factor in the aircraft becoming lost.

On the other hand, the possibility that it had been on an operational flight against the British Isles cannot be entirely excluded. Either way, the aircraft was abandoned over France and unexpectedly flew back across the English Channel to the English coast.

History does not record the names of the four airmen involved, but searches for them continued across a considerable period and employed soldiers, the Home Guard, Police and other volunteers as the hunt for them expanded.

Allegedly, the local hunt, riding to hounds, was also brought in to assist the widespread search. All that was achieved, though, was to exercise horse and hound.

Eventually, after many days, the frantic search was wound down, it being concluded that the crew must have fallen dead at remote locations and had not yet been located.

For the RAF, the mystery as to what had happened to these four airmen endured to the end of the war in what was then an inexplicable puzzle of the Blitz. ∎

Right On the morning of 28 November 1940, investigators swarm over the wreckage of the Luftwaffe's *'Marie Celeste'*, the abandoned Junkers 88 which landed itself at Blindley Heath in Surrey. Its crew had baled out safely over France.

Objects from the Blitz

The Blitz on Britain gave rise to scores of objects associated with the nation's struggle on the Home Front. We present a representative selection of items illustrating objects which will have been familiar to anyone living in Britain between 1939 and 1945.

PROPAGANDA POSTER

Despite its important role, the Ministry of Information was only officially formed the day after the outbreak of war – and it showed. Headed by Minister of Information, Hugh Macmillan, the Ministry was responsible for propaganda in film, radio and print. Perhaps due to inexperience and a rushed nature, the Ministry's first poster campaign backfired, becoming an object lesson in how not to make friends and influence people. Their very first poster – YOUR COURAGE, YOUR CHEERFULNESS, YOUR RESOLUTION, WILL BRING US VICTORY - was meant to boost public morale.

1. Identity Card

The National Registration Act, passed two days before the outbreak of war, made it compulsory for all Britons to carry proof of identity, leading to the issue of 46 million identity cards. It was impossible to obtain food or clothing without the card which carried details of marital status, name, age, gender, occupation and address and, most importantly, an individual national registration number. This was the 'smart' part of the card: rather than just random digits, the number identified a family household, even in which locality the holder lived. However, despite the relative sophistication of this numeric system, and as an immediate form of identification, it was seriously lacking in efficacy as most cards did not possess a photograph of the bearer. Members of the public were expected to carry their cards at all times. Although the war ended in 1945, the identity card scheme remained in force in attempts to counter the black market and those avoiding National Service. It was only abolished in May 1952.

2. Evacuee Label

There are several million people today who can thank a single government policy for their existence: that policy was evacuation. Realising cities would potentially become air raid targets, plans were made in 1938 to remove the most vulnerable from these built-up areas. On 1 September 1939, under Operation Pied Piper, city children were identity-labelled and escorted in groups to railway stations. In the first three days, 1.5 million Britons were evacuated, comprising 827,000 school children, 524,000 mothers and babies, 13,000 pregnant women, 70,000 disabled people and over 103,000 teachers and helpers. This evacuation identity label was for a 14-year-old schoolgirl who lived in Prestwich, just north of Manchester. She was evacuated with her classmates of Notre Dame High School to Blackpool, about 50 miles away – not too distant from her home and by the sea. The coastal resort became home to 35,000 evacuees, mostly from Manchester, but also from Merseyside and even as far away as London.

3. Black-Out Vehicle Headlamp

Bomber crews relied on visual targeting to aim their bombs and to hide conurbations at night and hinder the enemy, black-out regulations were introduced two days before the outbreak of war. A variety of measures were introduced: windows and doors had to be 'blacked-out' with dark material or boards, streetlights were doused and vehicle headlights fitted with filters, such as this Hartley headlamp device.

ARP LAPEL BADGE

Despite a common misconception that the ARP (Air Raid Precautions) organisation were Dad's Army-esque Warden Hodges-type amateurs, this was far from the truth. The key to the success of Britain's wartime ARP organisation lay in its early pre-war inception in 1924, allowing 15 years of planning. Often criticised as overly bureaucratic, governmental organisation had in fact acted early enough and, in doing so, saved millions of lives. Although overwhelmingly an amateur force, ARP personnel were mostly dedicated and professional, knowing their local sectors and residents inside out. They had extensive training, sitting courses and examinations in ARP proficiency and attaining relevant qualifications. Although Wardens are the recognisable 'face' of the ARP, there were various branches of the service, including: Rescue, First Aid Parties, Decontamination, Report and Control, Ambulance, Messenger etc. From 1941, it was renamed Civil Defence. The ARP, however, were local guardians who earned their place in wartime history.

4. Fire Service Hose

Designed for limited peacetime fires, Britain's pre-war fire brigades were insufficient for the huge challenge of wartime conflagrations. From 1939, the core of regular firemen at a main fire station were supported by Auxiliary Fire Service crews at new sub-stations, often located in evacuated schools or garages. Side by side, both professional and amateur firefighters faced an ordeal by fire. They drove out during the height of the raids to the epicentre of an attack. Exposed in the street or up high ladders, the only weapon they had in the face of the enemy were fire hoses, such as this genuine Blitz example. Made of heavy canvas, it also has a branch (or nozzle) made of brass to prevent any sparks igniting gas leaks. During the war, 793 firemen and 25 firewomen lost their lives, with another 7,000 seriously injured. Today, Britain's wartime firemen are largely forgotten heroes. How many lives and how much property they saved is incalculable.

5. German Bomb Splinter

The Luftwaffe employed a variety of weights of high-explosive (HE) ordnance, from 2kg anti-personnel bombs to their largest, the 2,500kg 'Max'. One glance at this fragment from a Luftwaffe 500kg HE bomb and instantly shows why it would prove lethal to any living being caught in its path. The jagged metal, still with its dark green paint, is from the bomb's tail-fin section. The bomb casing would shatter into hundreds, if not thousands, of pieces of red-hot metal splinters, pictured left. These splinters were blasted at the same speed as the gas expelled from the explosion, the detonation velocity being alarming: up to 10,300 metres per second, meaning

those in the way would have no chance of taking avoiding action.

6. Wartime Cookery Book

With limited food available, even the most inventive of cooks were challenged. But the Ministry of Food came to the rescue with leaflets, newsreels and a popular early morning five-minute BBC radio programme, 'Kitchen Front'. Broadcast from London, and hosted by Stuart Petre Brodie Mais, the show gave quick food tips and recipes. This booklet, published in 1942, contains some unusual delicacies: Black Pudding Hot-Pot, Baked Stuffed Sheep's Hearts, Roast Calf's Head and Wartime Canary Pudding – although no canaries were involved. Instead, custard powder gave it its yellow colour. The publishers noted: 'Our thanks are also due to Fougasse for designing the cover, but we warn our readers that this is not to be taken literally as a method of saving fuel!'

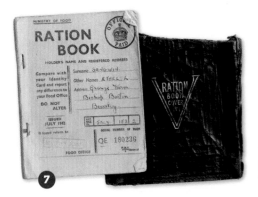

7. Ration Book

Whilst being an island has defensive benefits, it also has its drawbacks. In the First World War, Germany used its U-boat submarines to blockade Britain, limiting imports and food supplies and leading to food rationing in 1917. As the clouds of war once again threatened, the government began to plan for rationing in 1936, printing and stockpiling ration books two years later. The government was also far quicker to implement a programme of rationing: on 8 January 1940, bacon, butter and sugar were rationed. Meat, tea, jam, biscuits, cheese, egg, lard, milk and canned and dried fruit rationing followed. The first issues required shopkeepers to remove small coupons from the ration book on the purchase of rationed food. However, this became too laborious and from 1941, coupons were stamped by the retailer. This 1942-1943 example from Beverley, East Yorkshire, has been well-preserved in a leatherette 'Ration Book Cover' bearing the 'V' for Victory symbol.

8. Looting Warning Poster

As has always been the case throughout human history, not everyone acted for the common good or adhered to the general ethos of what was supposedly the 'Blitz Spirit'. Those who had not cared for the sanctity of other people's homes, shops or property before the war did not suddenly change their ways in September 1939. For the criminal minority, the war was not about pulling together: on the contrary, they saw it as a great opportunity for personal and illicit rich pickings. Indeed, though largely unknown today, recorded crime rose by 57%, from 303,771 offences in 1939 to 478,000 in 1945. This rare surviving post-raid poster, issued by the West Riding Constabulary, is a reminder of the less palatable side of British society that existed on the Home Front: neighbours were known to loot from neighbouring homes which had been destroyed or the families 'bombed-out'. Though decreed by law, the statutory punishment was

never carried out for this offence but was intended as a strong deterrent and the ultimate penalty.

9. Air Raid Shelter Sign

Implementing the government's national shelter policy, local councils built a variety of brick and concrete communal surface shelters in streets along with covered trench shelters, both types holding around 50 people. Neither type was bomb-proof but offered protection from blast and splinters. The shelters were designed pre-war with short, sharp air raids in mind: as it was, those sheltering sometimes had to sit on uncomfortable benches for hours on end as Luftwaffe raids often lasted most of the night. If the sirens suddenly sounded whilst civilians were out in the streets, this sign could well have saved your life. With white lettering on a black background to aid visibility in the blackout, such directional signs to the nearest air raid shelter were affixed to walls and lamp posts. Made of enamel – a melted and fused crushed glass finish on a metal backing – various similar signs were produced, including 'Gas Cleansing Station', 'First Aid Post' and 'ARP Report Centre' etc. all becoming familiar sights on the high street. As seen elsewhere in this publication, Air Raid Shelter signs were also frequently painted onto walls and buildings.

THE DEFENCE MEDAL

On Britain's Home Front, 60,595 civilians were killed by enemy action, with at least 86,182 injured. Of these, 2,379 ARP/CD, Police and fire service personnel were killed, with at least 4,459 seriously injured. Those who served on the Home Front, either in a civil or military capacity, were entitled to a medal with a ribbon of three colours. Designed by King George VI, the ribbon had a central flame-coloured orange band representing the fires of the Blitz, two thin black bands representing the black-out and a green background representing Britain's 'green and pleasant land'. However, the 1939-1945 Defence Medal is often overlooked and viewed as less important than campaign medals issued for service on other fronts. This should not be the case and the Defence Medal's significance should be reappraised: its recipients also served, fought and often died on what was the Home Front.

10. Civilian Gas Mask

Gas masks, or more officially, respirators, are perhaps the most symbolic and evocative objects of the Home Front, produced in vast numbers, yet ironically - and fortunately – they were never needed during the six years of conflict. The fear of chemical warfare was a legacy from the previous world war, which worried both the government and populace. As such, the first ARP measures largely concentrated on countering this grim menace. The Chemical Defence Experimental Station (now the Defence Science and Technology Laboratory) at Porton Down, Wiltshire, was tasked with developing gas masks that were economical to manufacture. By the war's end, a staggering 97 million General Civilian Respirators had been issued. Reflecting the number that were made, 80 years on, wartime gas masks still turn up quite regularly today.
Note: Though interesting and poignant relics, they should never be worn because their filters contain harmful asbestos.

11. House of Commons Rubble Souvenir Paperweight

The final attack of the London Blitz on Saturday, 10 May, 1941, would be a night that went down in London's history as a night of terror. With some 685 Luftwaffe bombers dropping almost 800-tons of bombs, that one attack alone killed 1,436 Londoners and injured 1,792 more. Many famous landmarks were hit, including Buckingham Palace, the Tower of London and Westminster Abbey. But the most famous casualty was Britain's historic cradle of democracy, the House of Commons Chamber, which was totally destroyed. Parliament was hit by 12 bombs, killing six officials. Creating a positive out of a negative,

London Stonecraft Ltd re-sculpted the Houses of Parliament's sand-coloured limestone rubble into different objects to raise funds for the Red Cross and St John Fund. Each piece came with a dated certificate. This example, a paperweight, bears a seal made from the roof lead of the Parliament buildings and shows the famous Clock Tower, known colloquially as Big Ben, and is dated 'London 1941'. Of note is that this piece retains the fire's blackened soot stains.

12. Stirrup Pump

It does not look the greatest war-winning weapon, but one should not be fooled by its appearance because this simple pump helped save Britain's towns and cities. A pump like this, the Hyrdropult, can be traced back to the middle of the 19th century: '...for washing, watering plants and extinguishing fires'. However, it would be in the next century that it saw its greatest service. Although devastating, incendiary bombs could be tackled by ARP firefighting parties with instructions issued for a team of three: one person pumping, a second lying on the ground directing the hose and a third supplying the pump bucket with water. It took up to six gallons to extinguish a single incendiary. By the war's end, some 3.8 million stirrup pumps had been produced. Amazingly, many are still in service with today's fire service: carried on appliances, they are particularly effective against chimney fires! ■

CHIEF AIR RAID WARDEN'S HELMET

New headwear was seen across wartime Britain and proved to be very popular – but this was no fashionable hat; instead, it was a protective steel helmet designed to save the lives of those working in air raids. Called a Mark II, it was based on a similar looking design introduced in 1915 during the First World War and called the Mark I helmet, but the basic design can be traced back as far as the 14th century - perhaps earlier. Produced in their millions, the Mark II was issued not only to Britain's military, but also its ARP, Police and fire services. Various initials, representing the wearer's branch of service, were added to the front, such as 'W' for Warden, 'R' for Rescue, 'A' for Ambulance and 'M' for Messenger, though a plethora of variations exist. Higher ranks wore easily identifiable white helmets with black bands. The example pictured belonged to John Merrifield, Chief Warden of the Earlsdon Division, Coventry.

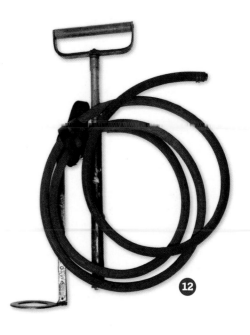

The German Bombs

During air attacks on Britain across the Second World War, the Luftwaffe employed a bewildering array of air dropped weapons. Some of them are examined here.

There were three types of German high explosive bomb dropped on the British Isles during the Second World War: thin-cased general purpose bombs (designated SC), thick-cased semi-armour piercing fragmentation bombs (designated SD) and the armour-piercing bomb (designated PC). The weights of these various types of bombs ranged from 50 kg up to 2,500 kg. The latter type was nicknamed 'Max', while the next size down was 2,000 kg followed by the 1,800 kg 'Satan' with the 1,000 kg nicknamed 'Hermann' – allegedly after the corpulent Luftwaffe commander-in-chief, Reichsmarschal Hermann Göring!

In a publication of this nature, it is impossible to cover the full range of types used by the Luftwaffe to attack Britain, but in terms of tonnage, high-explosive bombs accounted for the large majority of bombs dropped on the country.

The smallest and probably the commonest high-explosive conventional bomb used over Britain was the 50 kg SC bomb and tens of thousands of this type of bomb were delivered. This bomb type could be carried in multiples on all the main German bomber aircraft, and as it was a blast bomb it was capable of inflicting high numbers of casualties arising from shattering glass from windows and from flying debris and splinters. Typically, around five German bombs still need to be dealt with in Britain each year. They are very often of

the 50 kg type, although larger types are not infrequently discovered.

On the other hand, the greater the weight of the bomb, so the numbers of bombs in those weight groups reduced. Thus, bombs of 1,000 kg or over were delivered on relatively few occasions.

Across the period of the Blitz in 1940 and 1941, it is estimated that some 12,000 tons of bombs fell on London alone and across 71 separate air attacks.

The fuzing arrangements for conventional German bombs was generally along the same pattern and saw either one or two side pockets in the bomb's casing which held the fuze or fuzes. These could be of impact or delayed action type, and with some of them incorporating anti-handling

Left What appear to be two 500 kg bombs captured at the point of release from the external bomb racks of a Junkers 88. Many thousands of such weapons rained down on Britain during the Second World War.
Above A Heinkel 111 delivers its mixed bomb load during an air raid over Britain.
Above Right It almost became traditional for ground personnel to chalk messages onto the bombs that were about to be dropped. Often, these were rude or poked fun at their enemy. One notable example seen on a large calibre bomb read 'An extra Havana for Churchill!'
Below Right These ground personnel have marked this bomb: 'Hermann Brand'.
Bottom Large calibre bombs of 500 kg or 1,000 kg and larger were often painted pale blue to match the underside paint of the aircraft which carried them. When aircraft were painted black for night operations, the bombs were often sprayed black, too.

measures to make neutralisation of the weapon more difficult and extremely risky for bomb disposal teams. (The usual system for arming the fuses is described in the section on the 50 kg bomb.)

Here, we look at some of the more commonly dropped Luftwaffe devices.

THE HERMANN BOMB

The 1,000 kg Hermann bomb was a particularly devastating weapon with a full 50 – 60% of the bomb's weight of high-explosive amatol and the blast and the damage arising could be devastating. Because of the weight of the bomb, and the relatively limited capacity of Luftwaffe's bombers, the Heinkel 111 and Junkers 88 aircraft types could only carry one (or at most two) of these bombs during the main Blitz period, and this ability also depended on the range to the target. The Dornier 17-Z, however, was not able to carry these weapons at all. Their size and bulk meant that they could only be carried externally, and the

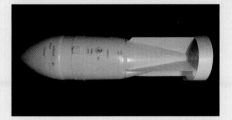

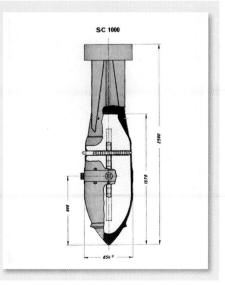

SC 1000

bombs were initially painted pale blue to blend with the blue under surfaces of the bomber aircraft.

However, as the Luftwaffe moved to night operations and started covering their aircraft with dull black paint, so the external bombs were sprayed a sooty black colour to prevent any reflective searchlight glare.

THE LUFTMINE

These large parachute-delivered weapons were originally intended for use at sea. However, they were adapted for use against land targets and were often known in Britain simply as Parachute Mines.

There were several types of Luftmine which weighed between 600 kg and 1,050 kg and these were all between 2 metres and 3 metres in length. The parachute slowed the Luftmine in its descent to around 40 mph on impact, the devices designed to settle on the surface of the ground and then explode. The explosive content was between 200 kg and 700 kg and the blast effect was huge, causing significantly more destruction across a greater radius than would a conventional bomb. If these weapons fell in residential districts, a single device could flatten houses over a very wide area. Many, however, failed to explode and were safely defused. A similar version was also used for maritime delivery, and it is not unusual for these devices to still be caught in fishing nets around Britain's coastal waters and requiring safe disposal by EOD teams.

Above A German Luftmine after it has been rendered harmless after being dropped on Glasgow on 18 March 1941.

Above A cargo of 50 kg bombs ready for loading onto a Dornier 17-Z prior to air operations over Britain. The 50 kg bomb was the commonest type of bomb dropped by the Luftwaffe over Britain.
Below Right This is a SD 50 version of the 50 kg bomb, its exact type denoted by the red tail cone. The aperture in the side of the bomb casing is the fuze pocket.

THE 50 KG BOMB

Although this weapon came in a variety of sub-types, the 50 kg bomb was the Luftwaffe's most frequently deployed conventional bomb. It was, in effect, the maid-of-all-work weapon and the SC 50 bomb had a 55% explosive content per overall bomb weight. These bombs were identified by a yellow stripe on the tail cone. Similarly, the SD 50 (which was used primarily against shipping or fortifications) had red stripe on the tail cone or had the tail cone painted entirely red. Because it had a thicker casing, the SD 50 had 35% explosive content per overall bomb weight.

Dropped in large numbers over Britain, the 50 kg bomb could be carried in multiple numbers by all German bombers. The Dornier 17-Z, for example, was capable of carrying 20 of these weapons. Inside the aircraft, the bombs were usually suspended vertically in a nose-up position and hung by a steel ring screwed into the nose.

As with all conventional air-dropped bombs used by the Luftwaffe, the fuze was located in a side pocket in the bomb, and this was electrically charged through a quick-release charging arm which disconnected when the bomb was released from the aircraft. Thus, the electrical charge initiated the fuze before the bomb was dropped, thereby rendering it 'live'.

THE BUTTERFLY BOMB

In many respects, one of deadliest of air dropped weapons during air attacks against Britain was the SD2 'Butterfly Bomb' – so called because the bombs were scattered from containers and the spring-loaded wings then opened and caused the bomb to flutter down. As they did so, the wings rotated up a cable shaft and armed the bomb through this twisting action. Thus, when the bomb landed, it was primed and would explode on the slightest vibration or if disturbed – although some were designed to detonate on impact.

Sometimes, civilians would accidentally trigger the weapons in the dark or if they were hidden in vegetation etc. In other instances, children were killed or maimed if they picked them up. Some versions of the bomb were painted yellow and had a vivid red stripe on the wings. The bright colours and strange appearance of the bombs often attracted the curious finder – frequently with deadly results.

They were virtually impossible to render safe and were often dealt with by firing at them from a safe distance with a .22 rifle. This method of disposal was almost always utilised in instances where the bombs had hung up on telephone or electricity cables, in trees or when caught on rooftops and guttering. However, three different fusing arrangements were used. One type detonated on impact (and could be deployed against troop concentrations etc.), another had a delayed fuse of between five and 30 minutes while the other detonated on disturbance. The latter was particularly hazardous, for obvious reasons.

The last known death caused by a SD2 bomb in Britain occurred in 1956, while a civilian in Malta was killed by one in 1981. Even today, bomb disposal teams deal with around three of these lethal devices every year in Britain.

THE OIL BOMB

Although these weapons were colloquially and popularly known as 'Oil Bombs' in Britain, they were in fact officially designated the Flammenbombe (literally, flame or firebomb) which came in the Flam C 250 (250 kg) or Flam c 500 (500 kg) versions – the latter was about 1.8 metres in length and contained around 150 kg of flammable material.

The weapons contained an oil mixture of 30% Benzine and 70% Petroleum and incorporated a high-explosive bursting and ignition charge. The bombs had a thin case, and very often the weapons failed to properly ignite and simply broke up on impact, thus spreading the incendiary contents widely instead of burning as was the intention.

As a result of their poor reliability, the bombs were used infrequently after the Battle of Britain period and were withdrawn in January 1941. However, when they worked as intended, they were certainly capable of spreading flammable material over a very wide area. If they fell into an already burning location, they would invariably increase the intensity of the blaze and potentially spread it further afield.

Above Such was the danger posed by Butterfly Bombs when they were used that the authorities went to great lengths to post warning notices in the areas they had been dropped.
Right The Flam 250 'Oil Bomb' was a large incendiary bomb but large numbers of failures with this bomb led to it being little used after December 1940.

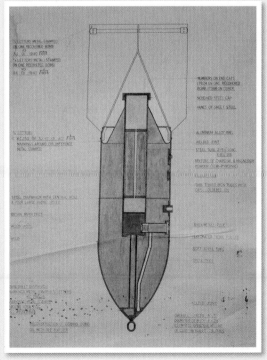

THE ENDURING LEGACY

With 20,000 tons of German bombs dropped on 16 of Britain's cities during the period of the Blitz alone, and with a percentage of those bombs failing to explode on impact, it is inevitable that unexploded bombs are still found on a very regular basis the length and breadth of the country.

Very often, UXBs were dealt with at the time, but this was only the case if the bombs could be reached safely – or at all. Sometimes, the presence of an unexploded bomb went undetected at the time it had fallen. This was especially the case during heavy air raids when the situation was often confused, and bombs could also penetrate very deeply into the ground. In these cases, the offending device could lay hidden for decades and only turn up when accidentally uncovered during construction work.

Today, 80 years after the Blitz, several such bomb discoveries are made every year and keep British military bomb disposal teams busy, requiring their operatives to be as fully conversant with German bomb types and fusing arrange-

ments as were their predecessors in 1941.

Since 2002, there have been at least 40 such discoveries in England and these have often been at locations associated with heavy air attacks. For example: Coventry, Southampton, Bath, Glasgow, Sunderland and Portsmouth. Of these 40 discoveries, 16 have been of 50 kg bombs – the remainder all being either 250 kg, 500 kg and 1,000 kg 'Hermann' bombs.

Of the latter, three discoveries have been made since 2008 when one of these massive devices was discovered during construction on the London Olympic site. In London's East End and Docklands area, the bomb had almost certainly been dropped during the 1940 – 41 Blitz period. Another 'Hermann' was found in 2015 in Coventry, almost certainly dropped during the Coventry Blitz on 14 November 1940.

Last, and during the production period of this publication, another was discovered in Exeter during February 2021. Again, this was a weapon which fell during Exeter's Blitz. This device had to be detonated in situ and the story made national and international news headlines.

Top The deadly legacy. This 250 kg bomb was discovered on a construction site in Kinston, Surrey, in 2019 and had to be detonated by the Army.
Above When a 1,000 kg Hermann bomb was discovered in Exeter in February 2021, it too had to be detonated in situ. This was the huge explosion resulting from its controlled destruction.

Firebomb Fritz

The most common Luftwaffe bomb used against Britain was the incendiary bomb
– a simple and yet devastating weapon dropped in many thousands against cities
and industrial targets.

At just one kilo in weight and 13 inches long, and when compared to bigger German high-explosive bombs, surely the incendiary bomb was the feeblest of all the weapons in the Luftwaffe's arsenal? In fact, it was one of the most devastating; a post-Blitz survey by British authorities revealing that for each ton of high-explosive bombs dropped, roughly 1¾ acres was destroyed. Whereas, for each ton of incendiary bombs dropped, at least 3¼ acres was destroyed.

The 1kg Incendiary used in the Blitz against Britain was officially the Elektronbrandbombe B 1 E, a design stemming from proposals by Griesheim-Elektron in 1917 to produce a magnesium alloy bomb with stabilising fins and a hollow body accommodating an incendiary filling. When a simple spring-loaded impact fuse ignited the contents, the case itself eventually combusted providing additional fuel for fire-starting. Essentially, this 1917 concept was the bomb which would rain down on Britain from 1940 until the war's end.

Production of the bomb had even reached a point during the First World War where Gotha bombers of Bombenfliegergeschwader 3 had been adapted to drop several thousand B 1 E Elektronbrandbombe (as they were then designated) each. The operational order had even been drawn up and had envisaged the creation of a large firestorm caused when they were dropped on London. In the event, no such attack was carried out - these tactics not materialising for another 22 years.

'TILE BUSTER'
Between the wars, Germany had been secretly testing new weapons and undertaking strategic thinking. As part of these preparations for war, the 1kg incendiary bomb came back into the frame as a potential weapon and trials conducted on the evacuated village of Schillersdorf in October 1935. It was found that the steeper the pitch of the roof on a building, the less chance existed for 1kg incendiary bombs to penetrate and start a fire in the roof space. Even so, most of the village was destroyed in the test.

Above When night became day. Fire fighters watch a burning London on the night of 16/17 April 1941 as incendiary bombs lay waste to large parts of the city.

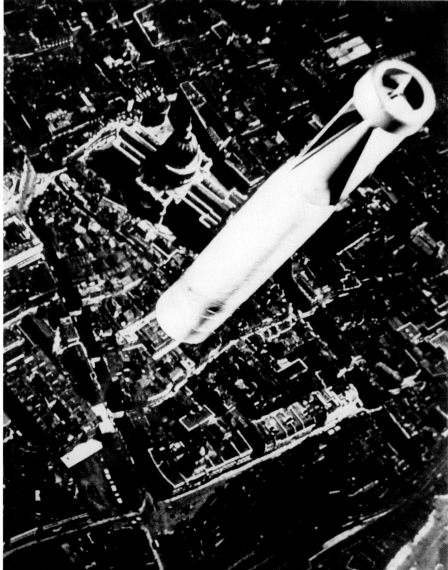

As a result of these trials, it was realised that if firefighting attempts could be hindered by the approach of a second wave of bombers dropping high explosive bombs, then the slow burning incendiaries gained more time for individual fires to take hold and spread. Incredibly, the weapon burned at 4,500 degrees Fahrenheit, a temperature sufficient to melt steel. The tests also highlighted a need for a better capacity for incendiary bombs to smash through tiles or slates.

As operations and their results were evaluated in the early months of the war, several versions of the B 1 E were developed including one, the B 13 E, which replaced the magnesium nose with a steel end increasing the weight to 1.3kg - hence its new designation. This enabled the bomb to more efficiently break through the tiles of a steeply pitched roof, hence its nickname: 'Tile Buster'.

Another version was the B 1 E Z, a standard bomb having the tail plug

removed and a steel collar inserted in its place to enable a fuse primer to be fitted.

This device was cunningly hidden by the tail fin of the incendiary, being invisible to those arriving to extinguish the bomb. Some two minutes after ignition, the heat generated detonated the charge with the intention of severely injuring or maiming, as well as further spreading burning material. This was intended to lead to wariness by firefighters approaching the burning incendiary bomb, thus giving conflagrations more time to build.

Facing Page Probably the most famous wartime public information poster in Britain was this example: 'Britain Shall Not Burn.' Presenting the incendiary bomb as 'Firebomb Fritz' it highlighted the huge dangers that this otherwise diminutive weapon presented.
Above Left The standard Luftwaffe 1 kilo incendiary bomb, designated the B 1 E.
Above Although the potential of these weapons had already been recognised by Britain's ARP service long before the war, this image of a German incendiary bomb superimposed above St Paul's Cathedral was particularly prescient. The huddle of buildings depicted around the cathedral were all but totally destroyed during the Blitz of 1940/41, much of the destruction being caused by incendiary bombs.
Left A favoured schoolboy souvenir of the Blitz was a set of fins from a burned-out incendiary bomb. With the bombs dropped in their thousands, these fins became regular playground 'currency' in swaps with bullet cases and shrapnel!

Beat 'FIREBOMB FRITZ'

BRITAIN SHALL NOT BURN

BRITAIN'S FIRE GUARD IS BRITAIN'S DEFENCE

ISSUED BY THE MINISTRY OF HOME SECURITY

PRINTED FOR H.M. STATIONERY OFFICE BY FOSH & CROSS LTD, LONDON (51/2033)

FIRE GUARDS

The Fire Watcher Service was initially formed in September 1940. However, during the Blitz many offices and buildings were left completely unattended, leading to incendiaries causing fires that could have been dealt with if detected sooner. In January 1941, a Fire Watchers Scheme was thus instigated, requiring that buildings in designated areas had to have a fire watcher present 24 hours a day. They were to deal with incendiaries as best they could and call on fire and rescue parties as required.

The Government implemented a compulsory scheme of fire watching, and Fire Guards, both men (aged 16-30) and women (aged 20-45), could be called up for duty. Volunteers were also accepted (men up to age 70, women up to 60). Generally, the duties on long nights were tedious and highly unpopular.

Fire Guards did not receive any official uniform but generally wore civilian clothes or a boiler suit. They would be issued with a helmet, armband, torch, means of dealing with small fires and a scoop for picking up incendiaries and a bucket of sand to put them out.

RUDIMENTARY IMPACT FUSE

In the 1940-41 Blitz, incendiary bombs were released in clusters of 36 from what were known as 'Molotov Bread-Basket' containers designed to swamp targets and making it harder for firefighters to tackle all the bombs dropped. Fortunately, due to a rudimentary impact fuze, a good proportion of incendiaries failed to ignite on landing. These were simply collected up by the ARP or by souvenir-hungry schoolboys!

Without doubt, these became some of the most common and popular souvenirs of the Blitz, along with the bomb fins from those missiles which had burned-out.

This device was one of the most destructive weapons of the Blitz. Such was its potential danger that householders were encouraged to remove all stored and potentially flammable material from loft spaces and to have buckets of sand and water available with widespread instruction

Top Teenager George Metacalfe on duty as a Fire Watcher at a factory in Upper Norwood, London, equipped with just a tin helmet, armband and torch with its blackout shield.
Above How a householder should tackle an incendiary bomb had been illustrated on a cigarette card as early as 1938.
Inset The 'Fire Guard' armband worn by the army of Fire Watchers.

given as to how best to extinguish burning bombs. This procedure had even been illustrated on a series of pre-war cigarette cards dating from 1938, anticipating what was to come.

Given the threat of incendiary bomb attack, and the damage these weapons could cause, there is little wonder, perhaps, that one of the most well-known public information posters of the war, issued by the Ministry of Home Security, was that depicting the incendiary bomb as a rather comically scary cartoon caricature: 'Firebomb Fritz'. ■

Operation Steinbock

Since the spring of 1941, London had been spared any large-scale air attacks.
All of that was to change on the evening of 22 January 1944 as the Luftwaffe
launched a mass attack which the British called 'The Baby Blitz'.

Just after 8.40 on the evening of 22 January 1944, around 447 bombers appeared over London in a massive raid as large if not bigger than any of the attacks of three years earlier. And it heralded a new phase of regular heavy attacks on London and other cities.

High explosive and incendiary bombs rained down on the city from an initial wave of 227 bombers. The skies blazing with searchlights and intense anti-aircraft fire and when the raid ended after just 30 minutes, Westminster was in flames; firebombs had struck Parliament, the Embankment, New Scotland Yard and other sites across the city. Then, just before dawn, a second wave of 220 bombers delivered another lethal payload onto the smouldering city.

By sunrise, nearly 100 Londoners lay dead, the hospitals full of casualties. It was the beginning of a deadly four months.

VENGEANCE TRUMPS PRAGMATISM

The English press dubbed the raids the 'Baby Blitz,' but to the Germans it was 'Operation Steinbock'. The campaign went down in history as the final Luftwaffe bomber offensive of the war - the brainchild of Reichsmarschall Hermann Göring as a retaliation to the Allied strategic bombing campaign against Germany.

Throughout late 1943, Göring lobbied Hitler to direct the Luftwaffe's dwindling bomber force to undertake massive retaliatory strikes on London. By pounding the enemy capital, he argued, the Allies would be deterred from future raids on German cities for fear of reprisal. Also, news that England was taking a beating would be pure gold for the Nazi propaganda machine. Others argued vigorously against the plan, maintaining

that Germany's limited air power needed to be preserved for use against an Allied invasion of Europe. Ultimately, the thirst for vengeance trumped pragmatism, and in November 1943 Goring's strategy was given the green light — German bombers would again fly over London *en-masse*.

To mastermind the campaign, 30-year-old General Dietrich Peltz was to implement operations. A veteran of more than 320 missions, the shortcomings were clearly evident to the General.

First and foremost, the Luftwaffe was not built for strategic bombing but for Blitzkrieg – tactical missions and close air support.

Undeterred, Dietrich Peltz stripped what aircraft he could from all fronts for the attacks and more than 500 aircraft were amassed for the operations.

A number of the new Heinkel He 177s were set aside for Steinbock. These

Left Operation Steinbock, or the 'Baby Blitz', between January and April 1944, was typified by heavy losses sustained by the Luftwaffe raiders. This is the wreckage of a Junkers 88 of KG6 brought down by a Mosquito at Withyham, Sussex, on the night of 24/25 February 1944.

Right By 1943, plans were being drawn up for the resumption of massed bombing attacks against London and around 500 aircraft were concentrated in France, Belgium, The Netherlands and Germany in readiness for these operations. One unit committed for these attacks was KG6 and one of its Junkers 88s is seen here at Creil, France, in April 1943, with Oberstleutnant Walter Storp (centre), Oberleutnant Rudolf Puchinger (left) and Major Hermann Hogeback. According to the original caption, they are planning an attack on Chelmsford.

Below Left In Essex, soldiers and an RAF airman are intrigued by the gun barbette from a Messerschmitt 410 which was brought down during the 'Baby Blitz'.

Below Right The human cost. On the ground, some 1,500 civilians had been killed and around 3,000 injured during the 'Baby Blitz'. This young boy has just been orphaned and sits dazed amid the ruins of his home.

were the only aircraft with bomb loads comparable to the B-17 or Lancaster. Although unreliable, they would be instrumental in the attacks.

MODERATE DAMAGE FOR HEAVY LOSSES

While the opening attack of 22 January rocked London, only about 30 of the 475 tons (about 6%) of bombs hit the city centre. Meanwhile, fighters and flak claimed around 25 aircraft, while 18 other bombers were lost. It was an inauspicious start to an operation to flatten London.

A follow-up strike was mounted a week later when 280 aircraft inflicted only moderate damage. Meanwhile, 28 Luftwaffe aircraft never made it home. Nevertheless, the operation continued, with missions ordered for 3, 13 and 18 February. The last of these raids saw a terrifying 186 tons of ordnance fall on the city, killing some 200 civilians.

Then, on 20 February, a 200-bomber mission, spearheaded by 14 Heinkel 117s, reached London with bombs falling all over Whitehall, with even 10 Downing Street suffering damage. More than 600 casualties were reported that one night.

More bombings continued into March, but the means did not justify the end, and while Hitler's bombers still managed to deliver deadly payloads onto the capital, the Luftwaffe was paying dearly. More

than 72 German aircraft had been lost in just the first month of the campaign alone. And those losses continued to mount.

UNMITIGATED DISASTER

The Luftwaffe continued with its London raids into April, while committing other bombers to sorties against Hull and Bristol. But while 1,500 civilians were killed, and hospitals choked with 3,000 wounded, Steinbock was clearly failing. As far as Berlin was concerned, it had been an unmitigated disaster.

Despite these raids, Allied bombers continued to pound Germany remorselessly. Worse, the Luftwaffe

squandered resources it could ill-afford to lose in a reckless gamble.

Of the 524 aircraft committed to the campaign, nearly 330 (or 60%) had been lost. This was a loss of one bomber and four crewmen killed or captured for every five people killed on the ground.

By the end of May, high command had finally called off the raids. But it was too late. The tactical blunder that had been Operation Steinbock had resulted in the Luftwaffe's bomber force being bled dry. Such were the losses that the Luftwaffe was unable to commit any truly viable bomber force to counter the Allied invasion of Normandy the following month. ■

Strange Finale

When a Messerschmitt 110 crashed into a Scottish field in May 1941, it coincided with the end of the main Blitz on Britain and saw the bizarre arrival of Adolf Hitler's deputy, Rudolf Hess. The event is an enigma which endures to this day.

At around 22.10 hours on 10 May 1941, the RAF's Chain Home radar system tracked an incoming aircraft heading for the Northumberland coast at a height of around 12,000 ft. It was hardly an unusual event for the period and the plot was designated 'Raid 42' by the RAF and passed, as a matter of routine, to 13 Group, RAF Fighter Command (the regional RAF air defence group), via RAF Bentley Priory in far-away Middlesex. Quite likely it was thought the aircraft was a solitary Luftwaffe reconnaissance machine, scouting out targets for the next assault on Glasgow or coming to assess previous raid damage.

The enemy was also picked up by a post of the Royal Observer Corps at a point seven miles NE of Alnwick, but what was unusual was that the aircraft lost height rapidly, crossing the coast at low altitude at around 100 to 50 feet. Once the aircraft passed inland, it became invisible to the seaward-looking radar and there was thus reliance on the Observer Corps to plot its track.

Once picked up by Observer Corps posts, observers initially suggested the unidentified aircraft might be a Messerschmitt Bf 110, partly given its speed. Although, for this area of the British Isles, such an aircraft type was way beyond its operational range. However,

one post eventually identified the aircraft visually in silhouette as it roared by, fast and low. It was indeed a Messerschmitt Bf 110.

At about 22.30 hrs it was still speeding across Scotland, although had climbed to around 5,000 feet, maintaining that altitude. The plot was then lost as it headed WNW across the Forest of Ettrick. Eventually, after crossing the forest, it was picked up again by observers at 22.45 hrs, still on the same heading. However, accurate sound plotting was now confused by an RAF Defiant flying in the same area - an aircraft that was airborne on the look-out for this solitary hostile machine.

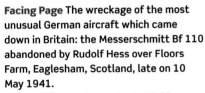

Facing Page The wreckage of the most unusual German aircraft which came down in Britain: the Messerschmitt Bf 110 abandoned by Rudolf Hess over Floors Farm, Eaglesham, Scotland, late on 10 May 1941.
Above Hitler photographed with his deputy, Rudolf Hess, in 1938.
Above Right An accomplished pilot, Rudolf Hess is shown here boarding a Messerschmitt Bf 110 of the type he flew to Scotland on 10 May 1941.
Below Right Collected from the crash site, the wreckage of Rudolf Hess's Messerschmitt Bf 110 is piled up at a railway goods yard awaiting disposal.

Shortly before 23.00 hrs, it was plotted briefly when crossing the west coast, but once over the sea it turned back inland on a reciprocal course before heading NE. Shortly afterwards, an observer post at Eaglesham reported it to have crashed at Bonnyton Moor, a few miles SW of Glasgow. Its pilot, meanwhile, had baled-out and was taken into captivity. He was the only occupant of the aircraft. Bizarrely, he also happened to be Hitler's deputy, Rudolf Hess.

In what was one of the strangest mysteries of the war, Hess secretly set off on a risky long-distance flight from Augsburg with a hare-brained plan to fly to Dungavel, the home of the Duke of Hamilton, to negotiate peace with the British. Although there is more mystery than established fact about the whole saga, the complex and seemingly nonsensical events have since been dissected and endlessly pored over.

PRISONER NUMBER SEVEN
After turning inland from the west coast, and with fuel running low, Hess prepared to bale-out by switching off both engines and feathering the propellers - although the starboard engine refused to stop and continued running until he throttled it right back.

Opening the cockpit, Hess undid the straps and tried to stand up to abandon the aircraft. However, the slipstream pushed him back, and with the aircraft in rapid descent he had to get out quickly if he was to survive. Pulling back on the control column, he tried to turn the aircraft on its back but blacked-out when the Messerschmitt entered a steep climb on the point of a stall. At this moment, Hess came-to.

Pushing with both feet, he managed to get clear as the aircraft stalled and fell away beneath him. Pulling his D-Ring, the parachute billowed open while the Messerschmitt dived to fiery destruction.

Right Rudolf Hess (right) at the Nuremberg War Crimes Tribunal where he was sentenced to life imprisonment. With him are Reichsmarschall Hermann Göring (left) and Großadmiral Karl Dönitz.
Below Right One engine from Rudolf Hess's aircraft is preserved by the Imperial War Museum, another is displayed at the Museum of Flight, East Fortune. This section of fuselage from the aircraft is also preserved at the Imperial War Museum, London.

Moments later, he landed in a meadow at Floors Farm, Eaglesham.

Initially, Hess passed out on hitting the field, but coming-to he was apprehended by a ploughman, David McLean. Mclean, asking if the parachutist was German, was astonished to get a reply in good English in the affirmative. The airman identified himself as 'Alfred Horn'.

The reason for his choice of assumed name remains a mystery - although those trying to unravel the whole conundrum have pointed to the fact that Hess's brother was called Alfred and that Horn was the name of his wife's stepfather, Karl Horn. Conspiracy theorists often point to the fact, too, that the initials A.H. were those of Adolf Hitler - but perhaps this is straying into the more surreal elements of the whole affair!

In Germany, Hitler reacted with rage, putting out statements about Hess's mental state and saying that 'hallucinations' led to his actions resulting from 'mental disturbance'. In the context of his mental condition, then German high command may well have been pretty much on the mark.

There is no merit in repeating here the various bizarre theories and suppositions regarding the episode, but once his identity was established, he was interrogated by British intelligence agencies and held as a prisoner in Britain before conviction at the Nuremberg War Crimes Tribunal. Here, he was sentenced to life imprisonment by the Allied powers.

To the Russians, life meant life and they would not consider early release. Instead, as 'Prisoner No 7', Hess remained incarcerated in Spandau Prison, Berlin, as its only prisoner, and guarded on rotation by the Russians, Americans, French and the British. During his imprisonment, there were even bizarre claims he was not really Rudolf Hess at all, but an imposter.

Controversy and mystery surrounded Rudolf Hess from the moment he took off from Augsburg until his death on 17 August 1987. Then, Hess supposedly committed suicide in the prison grounds

by strangulation with electric flex. Even in death, the Hess story was mired in controversy with unproven suggestions that the 93-year-old was too frail to have committed suicide and that he must have been murdered.

It would not be strictly true to say that the Hess affair was stranger than fiction; more accurate to describe it as being just as strange as fiction, because a popular novel of the period was *The*

Flying Visit by Peter Fleming, a tale where Adolf Hitler parachutes into England to try to make peace. Such a notion, or anything remotely like it, was the stuff of fantasists. And yet here was Hitler's own deputy doing pretty much exactly that.

Whatever the truth of the story, the arrival of Rudolf Hess rather strangely coincided exactly with the end of what is officially the Blitz proper: 7 September 1940 to 11 May 1941. ■

German Jets Over Britain

By early 1945, the war was all but lost for Germany. Nevertheless, the Luftwaffe was still able to brazenly operate its latest jet technology over Britain.

Development in technology had come a long way since the first air attacks against the British Isles had seen the implementation of Zeppelin airships and Gotha bi-plane bombers. By 1944, the Luftwaffe had its latest state-of-the-art aircraft available for air operations over Britain: the Arado Ar 234 B-1 jet.

From mid-1944, German air activity over the British Isles was limited and often comprised reconnaissance sorties flown by the new Arado 234 B-1, the only type in service with the Luftwaffe with the range to reach Britain and an ability to overfly it with impunity at speeds of 450 mph and altitudes of 30,000 feet.

From early August 1944, the type flew reconnaissance sorties over the Normandy invasion area from its base at Juvincourt, France. That same month, an Arado 234 B-1 was flown over Britain for the first time and used to photograph airfields in the south.

As the Allied advance moved inexorably forward, so the Arado 234 B-1 unit, Kommando Sperling, was forced to re-locate to Rheine, Germany, from

where it still had the range to reach Britain. For example, on 5 October, a two-hour mission was flown to photograph shipping in The Wash as well as RAF and USAAF airfields in Lincolnshire and East Anglia. The next day, another sortie was flown over SE England – these flights being long and lonely for the pilot, the only crew member.

By early 1945, Kommando Sperling was re-designated 1./Aufklärungsgruppe 123 and continued its operations over the British Isles. For example, on 24 February 1945, an Arado 234 B-1 approached Hull, banked to port and flew at high speed down the east coast of England photographing shipping, vessels in the Thames Estuary and the main sea supply route across to Antwerp. Here, it also photographed damage caused to the port by German V1 and V2 attacks.

Although no Arado 234 flights over Britain were ever intercepted or brought down, they were operations fraught with problems due to the unreliability of the Junkers Jumo 004 engines. However, the Allies were keen to get their hands on an example of the aircraft to study its jet

technology and when Hauptmann Josef Rigler of 9./KG76 suffered a failure of one engine in an Arado 234 B-2 and was forced down by a P-47 Thunderbolt at Selgersdorf, just inside Allied lines, the Western Allies finally got their hands on one.

Incredibly, the last Arado 234 B-1 sortie was flown over Britain in April 1945, just days away from the war's end. By then, its secrets were already in Allied hands and other examples were captured intact as Luftwaffe airfields were overrun.

Too late to make an impact on the course of the war, the introduction of the Arado 234 'wonder weapon' meant that German air operations over Britain spanned the airship age through to the jet age and had seen the introduction of the first unguided 'cruise missile' (the V1 Flying Bomb) and the V2 rocket. ∎

Above A captured Arado 234 B-1 jet is prepared at its German airfield in 1945 for a test flight by the RAF. The aircraft type had been flown operationally over Britain from the summer of 1944 right round to April 1945.

'Diver! Diver! Diver!'

Just as the Normandy invasion was getting into its stride, the Germans launched their V -Weapon campaign against Britain in what was to become a terrifying ordeal for the population of London and South-East England.

A ll told, and despite encouraging news from France following D-Day on 6 June, the summer was a terrifying one for those on the ground in southeast England. It was a terror that began on 13 June 1944.

Sitting in their Royal Observer Corps post atop a Martello Tower at Dymchurch on the Kent coast, two observers heard an odd and loudly rasping sound approaching from over the English Channel. Peering seaward, with binoculars scanning the skies, they spotted a strange flame '...like a gas

jet' rapidly heading towards them. In moments, they realised what it was and called 'Diver! Diver! Diver!' to their ROC Control Centre.

'Diver' was the codename previously allocated to these weapons, with British intelligence already knowing of their existence and being aware of the launch sites being built in northern France which had been spotted by RAF photo reconnaissance aircraft. As a result of those discoveries, the Air Ministry had alerted the Observer Corps to look out for them.

NAMING OF THE BEAST

The V1, or Vergeltungswaffe 1 (Retribution Weapon 1), was the forerunner of the modern cruise missile. The official designation of the weapon was Fi. 103, or Fiesler 103 - the airframe being manufactured by the Fieseler company. A cover designation of F.Z.G. 76 was devised by the Germans, this being Flakzielgerat, or 'target device for anti-aircraft', suggesting it was a training device for gunners. The development project's code-name, however, was Kirschkern (Cherry Stone) and the weapon known as

Left A V1 mounted on its launch ramp aligned directly towards London. This is at the preserved V1 launch site in the Forêt d'Eawy, France.

Above A V1 flying bomb is wheeled out in preparation for launching. The first of these weapons was intended to be sent against the United Kingdom at 23.15 hours on 12 June 1944, though this was delayed for operational until 03.30 hours the following morning when the order for attacks to begin was received by the battery commanders in the Pas de Calais. Ten flying bombs were launched; five crashed immediately, one came down in the sea, whilst the remainder droned on across the Channel.

Above The first V-1 launched at the United Kingdom was spotted by two members of the Royal Observer Corps – E.E. Woodland, seen here on the left, and A.M. Wraight, on the right, from their post on a Martello Tower at Dymchurch. When not on duty, they were a greengrocer and builder, respectively.

Maikäfer. Thus, it had had a bewildering range of designations attached to it. However, it became a Vergeltungswaffe after the Allied bombings of German cities, particularly of Hamburg in 1943.

The Allies, meanwhile, also had a variety of names for the device: Doodlebug was favoured by British civilians, probably driven by the popular press, and Buzz Bomb was particularly used by the Americans. Official records, however, often noted it as a 'P.A.C.', an abbreviation for a 'pilotless aircraft' or sometimes they called it a 'Fly', which was just a shortened version of flying bomb. The RAF, however, referred to it by the codename 'DIVER', doubtless due to the final act of its delivery. Later, the RAF would just refer to it as the Flying Bomb.

With a weight of 2,180 kg, standing 1.42 metres tall, a length of 8.36 metres and a wingspan of 5.38 metres, the V-1 carried an 830 kg warhead. The propulsive force was an Argus 109 pulsejet motor, fuelled by 600 litres of 75 octane petrol. The pulsejet engine gave the device a raucous buzzing sound and a tongue of flame projecting from its rear. The body, wings and pulsejet engine housing and the rear orifice pipe were manufactured from welded steel sheet, although later units incorporated plywood, especially for the wings.

With a range of 250 km (160 miles), it flew at a height of between 600 to 900 metres (2,000 to 3,000 feet) and at a maximum speed of 640 km/h (400 mph). Compressed air was used to pressure the fuel tank and to drive the gyros and control surface actuators.

A small propeller-driven counter determined how far the unit flew, and when a pre-set count was reached, two detonators were automatically fired. This blew out a wedge plate holding a lever under spring tension, and the release of the lever performed three actions: a cutter severed the air pipe to the rudder,

Above Just coming into service at the time of the V1 menace was the first RAF jet fighter – the Gloster Meteor. It had sufficient speed to catch the weapons, although the first one downed by a Meteor on 4 August 1944 was not actually shot down. When the aircraft's guns jammed, Flying Officer 'Dixie' Dean flew alongside the V1 and tipped it over with his wing tip, sending it down to crash and explode at Headcorn, Kent. It was the world's first aerial success by a jet fighter.

Right A Hawker Tempest in pursuit of a V1 over the English countryside. (The V1 is ringed in red) By March 1945, when the latter stages of the aerial V1 bombardment had finally ended, a staggering 10,000 flying-bombs had been launched. This included 1,500 launched from the aircraft after the main campaign against southern England ended in October 1945.

a claw locked the elevators in a down position and two small flaps dropped down underneath to act as air brakes and induce the dive.

The V1 was launched from a ramp (see heading photograph) precisely aligned to the target, and this incorporated a steam catapult to assist its launch.

With the capture of the launch sites in northern France, however, Heinkel III bombers were later used (to a limited extent) to air-launch the missiles. Used as a ramp launched device, the V1 was relatively accurate, but as an air launched device it was extremely inaccurate.

TWELVE SECONDS TO IMPACT

The original intention was that the dive would be made under full power. However, the nose down action caused fuel to surge to the top of the tank and this stopped the pulse jet motor. The stopping of the motor in this way resulted in the civilian population believing that 'Doodlebugs' simply ran out of fuel before crashing down indiscriminately. This inaccurate belief is often still repeated as fact, but it is incorrect.

The long gliding dive to impact could take some 12 seconds, giving those on the ground much anxiety as they knew

that for as long as one could hear the motor then one was safe. But when it stopped, those below it became potential victims. An anxious count might then take place by those who had taken cover, fervently hoping they would get to count to at least 13 or 14 seconds!

The target was always London, apart from air launched volleys against Southampton and Manchester, meaning that an area between Dover and Newhaven formed a triangle pointing to London over which the flying-bombs flew from their launch sites. All the flying bombs brought down before reaching London were the result of Allied countermeasures, which included an early inland organisation of anti-aircraft artillery, the 'Diver Gun Belt', running for 39 miles in a line protecting London to the south, and with a balloon barrage as a final defence protecting the city. In front of this defensive screen, towards the coast and across the Channel, RAF aircraft had free reign to intercept incoming missiles.

A major re-organisation from 14 July saw the anti-aircraft barrage re-located to the coast in a massive defensive system running continuously along the incoming flight path. This proved to be a master stroke of success, particularly with the

introduction of proximity fuzed shells and radar gun-control. The massive artillery barrage thrown up was described as a 'huge black curtain'.

Patrolling aircraft operated far out over the sea in front of the guns, and then inland between the AA defence line up to the balloon barrage curtain before London. This inland area was patrolled by pairs of aircraft flying defined and co-ordinated circuits across the whole region, waiting for incoming V1's identified by sight or indicated by warning rockets fired from the ground or else by being controlled onto targets by radar.

Only a handful of aircraft were fast enough to achieve the speed necessary to mount attacks on the V1 which flew at an average speed of 345mph but were capable of up to 400 mph. Alongside the Hawker Tempest and Typhoon, the Gloster Meteor jet was just coming into service with the RAF's 616 Squadron at Manston and later mark Spitfires, night-flying Mosquitos, Beaufighters and the North American P-51 Mustang were all being used. Some aircraft were modified to boost engine power with water-methanol injection, polished to reduce drag and their weight reduced by removing unnecessary equipment and painted to boost speed. For the flying bomb and the pursuing aircraft, flight time from the coast to the balloon barrage amounted to around eight minutes.

'BOMB ALLEY'

Initially, many members of the public thought the V1s to be aircraft in trouble passing overhead and on fire. But it wasn't long before people were quickly disabused of that notion! Within days, examples of the fearsome missile were falling the length and breadth of Sussex and Kent and onto London itself, almost non-stop in a continuous 24-hour salvo. Day in, day out. For the *most* part, the track of the Flying Bombs took them over routes across East Sussex

Top One that got through – a V1 flying bomb in the last few seconds of its flight before it fell on to the streets and buildings of London somewhere in the vicinity of Piccadilly station.
Above German propaganda leaflets of the period fed into the fear felt by the British population during the height of the attacks.
Right This frame of images from an RAF fighter's camera shows how dangerous it was to shoot these weapons down, the attacking aircraft invariably flying through a cloud of exploding and white-hot debris.

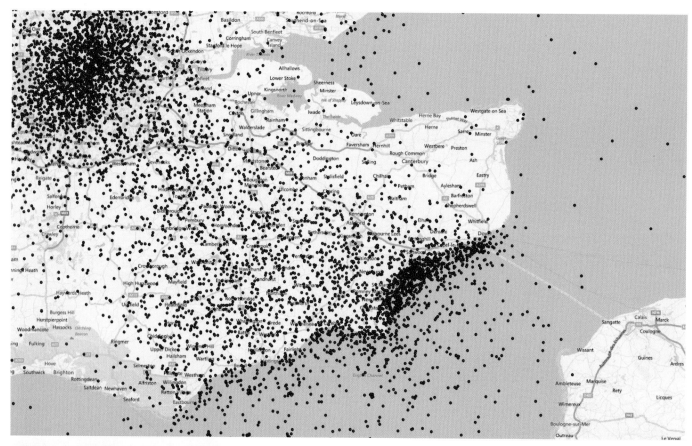

Above This map of London and southeast England shows all V1 impact points during the campaign which stretched from June to October 1944. In total, 9,521 of these missiles struck London and the Home Counties. (CREDIT: @CraterLocators)

Left As a schoolboy, Ken Munday watched in horror as a fighter brought down a V1 over the East Sussex village of Westfield, the bomb landing on a cottage and killing its occupant, a young lady called Doris Lynch. Doris was eight months pregnant, and Ken has looked after her grave ever since. Originally unmarked, the grave now has a marker bearing her name and the brief details of her death.

Below Left Today, a tree stands close to the impact point of the V1 flying bomb which fell at Headcorn. Scarred with splinters from the blast, the tree is remarkably still living!

and West Kent. And although there were plenty of flying bombs which flew (and fell) either side of this swathe of countryside, this was by-and-large the heaviest concentration. Little wonder that it became known as 'Bomb Alley'.

For the British authorities, of course, the attacks came as no surprise and defensive measure were quickly instigated. Once established, it became an effective defensive belt to try to prevent as many of these missiles as possible reaching London, their intended target. Out to sea, as the RAF fighters patrolled and tried to intercept the fast-flying VIs – with Spitfires and Tempests primarily engaged in the interception role. However, shooting at them with 20mm cannon, and at close range, was a hazardous occupation if the warhead detonated. In fact, a considerable number of RAF pilots were killed when this happened. Very quickly, RAF pilots learned a new trick – to fly

alongside, edge a wing under the VI and literally flip it over. This process toppled the gyroscopic controls and sent the bomb down to destruction. Over the sea there was little or no risk of death, injury or property damage. Overland, and it was a different matter.

Sadly, this all meant that those living in the areas between the south coast and the south London suburbs were in danger when the VIs were intercepted and brought down. And a very considerable number of deaths and injuries inevitably resulted. However, a cold calculation had had to be made: if they could be downed before reaching the dense population of London, then the loss of life would likely be lower.

It was a grim decision to have to take, but in fact the vast majority of VIs downed over Kent and Sussex did fall harmlessly in open countryside, farmland, woods, and forest. But not all, of course. Additionally, not all the bombs

Above On 30 June 1944, a V1 exploded on the roadway in Aldwych, London, causing the utter devastation seen here and resulting in the third largest death toll of the flying bomb campaign. In total, 48 people died and 150 were seriously injured.

were brought down by defensive action. Some just fell when the motors cut out.

Sometimes, though, the results of RAF interceptions were almost comical, and one witness told of hearing an approaching Flying Bomb as she was out with her baby daughter, shopping in the East Sussex market town of Hailsham. Looking to the south, and towards the expected approach, she could see nothing. Suddenly, she realised the sound was approaching from behind her – the VI travelling from north to south. Either side, escorting it, was an RAF Spitfire. "How we cheered!" she recalled.

Sometimes, though, the results of such interceptions were tragic rather than comic. Again, on another occasion, the same witness watched as a RAF fighter downed a VI to the south of Hailsham:

'There was a terrific explosion, and we just hoped it had fallen harmlessly. Sadly, it hadn't. It fell at a farm called Mulbrooks, killing a Land Army girl and farm worker when it tipped over a haystack. Both of them were suffocated, I believe. It was terrible, really.'

Similarly, a fighter downed a VI over Westfield, just to the north of Hastings in July 1944, and instead of falling in the vastness of open countryside around the village, it fell directly onto a solitary cottage killing the only occupant - a young woman who was eight months pregnant. It was just thoroughly rotten bad luck. She was, though, the only casualty in the small parish which, astonishingly, had no less than fourteen flying bombs downed within its boundaries.

The VI campaign had been terrifying and deadly. Between 13 June and the end of the campaign in the late summer, many thousands were launched against Britain. Of these, 2,340 had hit London, causing 5,475 deaths and resulting in 16,000 others being injured, many of them seriously.

Damage to property had been extensive, although it can be argued that the weapons had little military value save for tying up defensive assets. However, the attacks certainly began to affect public morale.

The VI, however terrifyingly destructive, did not change the course of the war. The German regime prioritised their new V-weapon resources - often over traditional warfare requirements - and there was already an inability by the Luftwaffe to adequately defend against the massed raids of Allied aircraft by day

THE V1 FLYING BOMB

The V1 was the first of the so-called 'Vengeance weapons' series (V-weapons or Vergeltungswaffen) deployed for the terror bombing of London. Developed at the Peenemünde Army Research Centre from 1939, during initial development it was known by the codename "Cherry Stone". Because of its limited range, thousands of V-1 missiles launched against England were fired from launch facilities along the northern French coast. The Wehrmacht first launched the V-1 to target London on 13 June 1944, one week after D-Day, and doubtless prompted by the invasion.

At the peak of the campaign, more than one hundred V1s a day were fired at south-east England, 9,521 in total, decreasing in number as launch sites were overrun until October 1944, when the last V-1 site in range of Britain was overrun by Allied forces.

Essentially, the V1 was the first cruise missile and was officially the Fiesler Fi 103.

It had a length of 8.36 metres (27.3 ft) and a wingspan of 5.38 metres (17.6 ft) with a warhead weight of 830kg (1,870 lb). It was powered by a pulse-jet motor and had a range of 250 km (160 miles) and operated with a gyrocompass autopilot system, flying at around 400 mph and altitudes of between 2,000 to 3,000 ft, although often much lower.

and night. These were raids, of course, which could drop almost as many tons of bombs in one 24-hour period as the whole VI campaign achieved in its entire duration. But that was little consolation to those on the receiving end of the 'Doodlebugs'.

Eventually, the attacks diminished before finally petering out when the launch sites in northern France and around the Pas-de-Calais were overrun. But what was to come next – the V2 campaign – was equally terrifying. ∎

'Big Ben'

Having endured the V1 Flying Bomb campaign, the population of Britain
was subjected to a new terror from September 1944: the V2 rocket.

At around 18.43 hours on 8 September 1944, two massive explosions rocked Chiswick and Epping. At Chiswick, the first of the two blasts, three people were killed and 20 injured, ten seriously. Sixteen seconds later, another massive explosion tore through Parndon Wood, near Epping, but caused no casualties.

To the public, there was no obvious explanation as to the cause; no enemy aircraft had been overhead and there was no air raid warning. However, the Allies had known for some while that V2 missile attacks were likely, although this had been kept from the British public. And since the first two strikes caused little more damage than a V1 Flying Bomb, the real reason for the explosions

was suppressed. Initially, this was in the hope that no more would follow – or, at least, that the launch sites in Holland would soon be captured and the menace neutralised.

Two days later, another rocket fell in Essex. Then, the following day, four more fell at Kew Gardens, Dagenham, Biggin Hill and at a location near Rochford. Progressively, across the rest of the month, the tempo of rocket strikes increased, and the casualty toll rose. Nevertheless, the public remained ignorant as to the cause of these huge blasts. As a cover, the government initially passed them off as gas explosions, cloaking each event in secrecy with a news blackout and giving them the codename of 'Big Ben Incidents.'

With the frequency of strikes, however, the cover explanation would no longer wash, although it was not until 11 November that the truth was finally revealed. By this date, 165 missiles had hit Britain – many with devastating results.

The particularly terrifying nature of V2 attacks was that they came without warning and there was no means to defend against them. In effect, the era of the Cold War Intercontinental Ballistic Missile (ICBM) had been born. On the other hand, it is worth noting that the designer of the weapon, Werner von Braun, was captured by the Americans in 1945 and went on to work for NASA where he masterminded the giant Saturn V rocket, thus enabling the American moon missions of the 1960s. Subsequently, his

role in the project – and the willingness of America to overlook his complicity in war crimes through slave labour – has been controversial.

DEVELOPING THE V2

Official German interest in rockets started in 1929, at a time when civilian enthusiasts were building and launching solid-propellant rockets as a hobby. Research was commissioned, quickly identifying that solid-propellant rockets were limited in range and that liquid propellants offered greater scope.

The first test firing of a liquid fuelled unit took place in 1932 at Kummersdorf firing range near Berlin, and in 1934 the launch of a small liquid fuelled rocket, the A2, was achieved from Borkum into the North Sea. Larger designs, the A3 and the A4, followed - the A4 later becoming the V2.

The A4 – or Aggregat 4 (Series 4) - had its first successful launch in October 1942, and a manufacturing, development and test centre established at Peenemünde on the Baltic coast. Bombing by the RAF of Peenemünde in August 1943 led to the dispersion of manufacture, with assembly transferred to a tunnel complex under the Harz Mountains near Nordhausen.

Originally Gypsum mines, the tunnels were identified in 1943 as suitable for armament production and enlargement of the tunnels began. This work utilised slave labourers who were kept underground 24 hours a day, many dying in appalling conditions.

Production of the A4 commenced in late November in the underground complex, now called Mittelwerk. At the northern (Nordwerk) Heinkel 162 jets were produced and the southern end of the complex was used for V1 Flying Bomb production.

PREPARATIONS FOR LAUNCH

Over 500 officers and men were required to launch a V2, these being split into three specialist troops:

The Fuel and Rocket Troop were tasked with off-loading the rocket and various fuels and chemicals from rail delivery points and transport to the assembly location for the rocket and transferring to the launch position the required fuels and chemicals.

The Technical Troop mounted the warhead and performed checks on the systems. They also carried out field repairs to ensure the correct function of the V2 and moved the rocket to its launch position.

The Launching Troop prepared the launch position and erected the rocket onto the launch table. Using optical devices, they ensured it was vertical. Further checks were performed, and the rocket fuelled.

The launch table contained a rotating ring enabling the V2 to be turned so that the number one fin was *precisely* aligned with the line of fire to the target. Optical devices were also used for this operation.

After preparation (which could take five hours), the launch position was cleared and the launch controlled from an armoured vehicle connected to the V2 with cables.

An igniter (an electrically initiated pyrotechnic on the end of a long pole) was then placed up into the combustion chamber. The launch would then commence, and the fuel, comprising four tons of ethyl alcohol and six tons of liquid oxygen, was released to the combustion chamber.

The 75% alcohol-by-volume fuel took over 25 tons of potatoes to produce and it could also be a potent drink. Consequently, measures were introduced to prevent consumption, such as the addition of purple dye.

Methanol was introduced later, and if drunk it had lethal consequences. But soldiers are ever resourceful and discovered that charcoal filters from gas masks produced drinkable results. It was, quite literally, 'rocket fuel' alcohol!

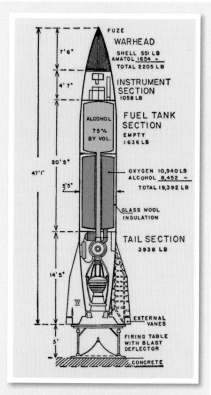

V-2 'A-4' Rocket Specifications

Mass	12,500 kg (27,600 lb)
Length	14 m (45 ft 11 in)
Diameter	1.65 m (5 ft 5 in)
Warhead	1,000 kg (2,200 lb); Amatol (explosive weight: 910 kg)
Detonation	Impact
Span	3.56 m (11 ft 8 in)
Propellant	3,810 kg (8,400 lb) 75% ethanol. 25% water. 4,910 kg (10,820 lb) liquid oxygen.
Range	320 km (200 miles)
Altitude	88 km (55 miles) maximum altitude on long-range trajectory 206 km (128 miles) maximum altitude if launched vertically.
Speed	Maximum: 5,760 km/h (3,580 mph) At impact: 2,880 km/h (1,790 mph)
Guidance	Gyroscopes to determine direction. Müller-type pendulous gyroscopic accelerometer for engine cut-off on most production rockets.
Launch	Mobile - Meillerwagen.

FROM LAUNCH TO IMPACT

With activation of the igniter, the fuel commenced burning but the thrust was less than the weight of the rocket. Thus, potassium permanganate and hydrogen peroxide were mixed to initiate a violent chemical reaction producing large volumes of steam. The steam was piped to a turbine, powering a pump for alcohol and another for liquid oxygen. So powerful was the pump that it could shift 10 tons of fuel in under a minute. With fuel under pressure, a thrust of

Top Left The test launch of a V2 rocket from Peenemunde.
Above A Policeman examines the combustion chamber from a V2 rocket which has bust in mid-air.
Bottom Left Londoners examine debris from a V2 rocket in a residential street.
Right This V2 is prepared for public display at RAF Biggin Hill during the 1960s. It is probably the same missile pictured in the lead illustration to this section. NB: One of the earliest V2 rockets fell at Biggin Hill on 10 September 1944.

25 tons was achieved to enable lift-off and connection to the launch vehicle disconnected. All aspects of function were now under the autonomous control of the rocket.

Beneath the warhead, and above the alcohol tank, a compartment contained the devices needed to provide control. The first four seconds of flight were vertically upwards, a timing circuit then triggering the main gyroscope to alter the pitch of the rocket to 47° from the vertical. Four graphite vanes in the rocket

Above Censors often deleted areas in newspaper photographs which would have given away clues as to precise locations. On this original print, the censor has marked in red the areas he wanted deleted. The photograph actually depicts the aftermath of a V2 strike on 8 February 1945 in Ilford which killed 14 and injured over 140.
Right As Allied forces went ashore on Terschelling Island, a V2 launch was observed headed for England, leaving its zig-zag vapour trail, the scene being captured by a war artist.

exhaust and small fin rudders provided steering holding it in a straight line.

When a pre-set velocity was reached, close of burn was initiated, the thrust moderated to eight tons for a few seconds and fuel valves were closed. In just over 60 seconds, the V2 accelerated to Mach 5 and was 35 km (22 miles) high. The rocket continued upwards to around 88 km (55 miles) before dropping back to earth in a parabolic curve. Falling back through the atmosphere created friction and heat, with temperatures on the steel skin reaching 640 °C.

The heat of re-entry could cause fuel tanks to explode and rockets to break up, but a solution was found by packing the space between the fuel tanks and external skin with glass fibre, held in place with chicken wire. However, break-ups still occurred.

The terminal velocity was between Mach 2.8 and 3, and on impact the rocket could be several metres into the ground before detonation.

The V1, meanwhile, carrying a similar sized warhead to the V2, glided down and detonated causing blast that spread over a large area because it did not penetrate the earth. The V2, though, penetrated to depth before exploding, creating a large crater, and channelling blast upwards.

A DREADFUL TOLL

A direct hit by a V2 was devastating and caused immense destruction. However, it was not accurate, and the mean point of impact was 10 km north-east of the City of London, the V2 not having the requisite precision to consistently hit the city or its suburbs. The spread of fall was in the order of three times greater than this area. As a result, many rockets fell on farmland, in woods or water. *(Note: many of these 'off course' rockets were launched at night, and it is thought that darkness may have impeded the necessity for extreme precision in setting the missile up for launch and thus the accuracy in targeting.)*

V2 construction consumed resources for the Germans that could have been used for the manufacture of conventional armaments, and with comparison between the cost of a V1 and V2 putting the V2 at 100 times the cost of the V1,

the drain on resources was 100 x greater for the delivery of the same amount of explosive.

By the end of the V2 campaign, 2,754 civilians had been killed and 6,523 seriously injured (mostly in London), there having been almost 2,500 rockets launched against Britain. On average, this equated to two fatalities per V2, and while some fell harmlessly in open countryside, others caused great devastation and resulted in far higher death tolls. For example, one V2 fell onto a Woolworth's

V2 - THE HUMAN COST

17/18 August 1943: RAF bombing of Peenemünde. 735 killed including 557 foreign workers, mostly Polish.

1943/1945: Construction of Mittelwerk and the assembly of V2 estimated to have cost the lives of 20,000 slave labourers, although the movement of many prisoners from concentration camps in 1945 to the area has added to the figures.

3 March 1945: RAF bombing of Bezuidenhout, Netherlands. 511 killed, 344 injured, 20,000 made homeless. Target was V2 assembly and storage, but a residential area was hit.

3/4 April 1945: RAF Bombing of Nordhausen killed 1,500 sick prisoners from Camp Dora who had been left to die at the Boelcke Kaserne barracks. (Over 7,000 people were killed in Nordhausen town).

V2 campaign against London: In total, 2,754 people were killed and 6,523 seriously injured. The first V2 struck London on 8 September 1944, the last on 27 March 1945.

V weapon campaign (V1 and V2 combined) against mainland Europe targets: 3,736 killed and 8,166 wounded. The largest loss of life in a single V2 impact being in the packed Rex Cinema, Antwerp, 16 December 1944, 576 killed, including 296 Allied servicemen.

Above On 27 November 1944, a V2 struck Antwerp killing 126 people including 26 British soldiers in a military convoy. This was the grim aftermath.

store at New Cross, London, during the afternoon of 25 November 1944, killing 160 and seriously injuring 108 people, the worst V2 death toll in Britain.

The last V2 fell on Britain on the morning of 27 March 1945, hitting Hughes Mansions on Vallance Road, Whitechapel, killing 134 people in an attack just weeks away from the end of the war.

As the Germans were pushed further back into Europe, so the launch sites from where London could be reached meant the attacks on Britain ceased

after 27 March. However, the Germans continued to launch V2s against targets in Europe in attempts to impede Allied advances.

Antwerp and its docks became a primary target, and in one attack 567 people were killed when a cinema there was hit.

The casualty figures exacted by the V2 campaign, and the death toll among those who built them, or who were killed during Allied attempts to disrupt rocket construction, was truly a terrible one. ∎

Traces of The Blitz

Given the pounding from aerial assault suffered the length and breadth of the British Isles, it is unsurprising that evidence of these events can still be found. In the Capital there are plenty of reminders of London's Blitz – often 'hidden' in plain sight.

Although the post-war clear-up of bomb damage was largely complete by the late 1960s, traces of the Blitz against Britain are still to be found if one knows where to look and what to look out for. On the south coast for instance, at Eastbourne and St Leonards-on-Sea, bomb splinter marks and bullet holes from Luftwaffe attacks are still plainly in evidence – including a bullet hole through a promenade railing at Eastbourne and another in the skirts of Queen Victoria's statue on the seafront at St Leonards-on-Sea. Doubtless, she was not amused! These are far from isolated examples.

Without doubt, the preserved ruins of Coventry Cathedral must be considered the ultimate symbol of Blitz remembrance. Preserved after the terrible air raid of 14 November 1940, it stands as a permanent memorial to that catastrophic event. And in the West Country, at Bristol's Arnos Grove Cemetery and at the city's St Nicholas Church, for example, bomb splinter impact marks are reminders of that city's dreadful ordeal. These are just a few reminders that the Luftwaffe once passed this way. It is in London, however, where the largest concentration of surviving evidence of bombing and various measures taken to implement air raid precautions still exists.

Around the Capital, a city so badly battered by air attack, it is not difficult to find many ghostly fingerprints of war. And while the city has healed, its scars remain. In many cases, the evidence would go unnoticed. For example, sections of brickwork varying from surrounding masonry, cryptically worded and fading painted signage, oddly squat brick buildings or gaps in a street's fine façade which are inexplicably filled with brutalist architecture. Quite likely, all are viewed as unremarkable and not given a second thought or another glance.

On the other hand, the evidence is sometimes stark: preserved ruins of bombed buildings, vicious bomb splinter marks in walls or monuments and camouflage paint still on buildings. All are seen in this photographic 'sightseeing tour' around London.

Left When the Blitz proper ended in May 1941, it was not entirely the end of the ordeal. London continued to be raided sporadically thereafter, culminating in the V1 and V2 attacks of 1944 and 1945. With extensive damage such as that shown here, it is perhaps surprising that there is not more evidence of the 1940/41 Blitz to be found around London.

BOMB DAMAGE

Although the bomb sites of the 1940s are now long gone, there are still remaining examples of bombed-out buildings to be found at London Wall in the City of London. The area was largely obliterated on 29 December 1940, and when the rubble was cleared, Roman remains were discovered beneath. To the City of London Corporation's credit, the Blitz-wrecked buildings were retained as part of the architectural montage and visitors can now see remnants of the Roman wall and fort, together with Blitz damage, all juxtaposed against present-day office buildings. Truly, layers of this great city's history.

Many noticeable examples of splinter damage can be found around London with some at Waterloo Place on the plinth of Lord Clyde's statue, St Clement Danes Church, and at the Science and V&A Museums in South Kensington. Here, as well as on the buildings on either side of Exhibition Road which are liberally showered with splinter damage, a red telephone box has its own war wounds.

1 Blitz ruins still standing over Roman archaeology, juxtaposed with modern architecture.
2 Bomb splinter marks on Lord Clyde's statue in Waterloo Place.
3 The wall of the V&A Museum is liberally peppered with heavy splinter marks from the detonation of a Blitz bomb. It is perhaps the most dramatic of the remaining bomb splinter damage examples in London.
4 'Are you there, caller?' Outside the V&A, this telephone kiosk bears its own scars of war.

SHELTER SIGNAGE

Air Raid Shelter signage remains in some places, too, although with the passage of eighty plus years they are gradually fading away. There are many examples in the City of Westminster, both the conventional 'S' for shelter type and more intricate designs informing of shelters in vaults under pavements etc. Bermondsey, Deptford and Southwark also show an impressive array of shelter signage, sometimes on local authority estates and occasionally on ordinary street corners, as can be seen, for example, at Frankham Street, Deptford.

Above Shelter Signs at 1 Frankham Street, SE8, 2 Upper Brook Street, W1.
Right The damaged W H Smith sign at London's Portugal Street.

SPLINTER MARKS ON SIGN

At Portugal Street, London, splinter marks on a sign marking the head office of newspaper distributors, W H Smith & Son, are tangible reminders of a night attack on Thursday, 10 October 1940. Oddly, the Home Office ordered that the Daily Appreciation Reports on the air attacks were not issued and thus no global report of the raids in that 24-hour period exist.

NFS PUMPING STATION

In Charlton, visible from the Thames Path, is probably the last remaining example of an Auxiliary Pumping Station, once used by the National Fire Service. Again, to the average passer-by, it would be an unremarkable piece of the industrial landscape and probably some long-abandoned pier or jetty. Based on experience gained early-on in the Blitz, a network of these stations was constructed along the Thames to be used for pumping river water into hydrants for use in fighting fires. This system was especially useful when the mains supply was damaged and trailer pumps could also be used to relay water to where it was required.

Right Looking like an abandoned jetty, this is the last remaining example on the River Thames of an Auxiliary Pumping Station at Charlton which was used to pump up water for the NFS and is an important but neglected piece of London's Blitz history.

STRETCHER FENCES

Once common across the capital, but still seen in southeast London, are examples of post-war recycling in the form of former ARP stretchers repurposed as perimeter fences at many local authority housing estates. These tubular steel and wire mesh stretchers were built in the hundreds of thousands in anticipation of mass casualties resulting from an enemy bombing campaign on Great Britain. Fortunately, casualties were nowhere near that which had been projected. The majority of stretchers now in use at various locations, such as these in Greenwich, probably never saw any usage let alone a casualty.

STOKE NEWINGTON TOWN HALL - CAMOUFLAGE

The Civil Defence control for Stoke Newington, north London, was located within the basement of the Town Hall, built in 1937. Perhaps because of its wartime use, it was decided to apply an RAF-style camouflage scheme across the whole structure in order to disguise it from the air. The painters obviously did a thorough job because the paint scheme can still be clearly discerned today, especially on the parts of the building that are less exposed to the elements as seen in this photograph.

AIR RAID WARDEN'S POSTS

The Air Raid Wardens system was controlled across the country on a municipal basis, responsible to the Civil Defence controller of each borough (usually the Borough Secretary) at the Town Hall and operating at a local level through a network of Wardens' Posts. Sometimes, these were located within existing buildings, but more usually were in purpose-built structures such as these, looking something like surface air raid shelters. There are examples of these to be found across the capital, such as that seen in this photograph at Blackfen, southeast London, and at Wallington, further south.

Above This rather ordinary and unremarkable looking brick structure at Wallington is, in fact, an ARP Warden's Post – a vital piece of Blitz infrastructure.

BOMBED-OUT CHURCHES

The Square Mile of the City contains the shells of three bombed-out churches; one of these is Christ Church Newgate which lies in the shadow of St Paul's Cathedral. There is also another bombed-out church in the south-eastern suburbs at Woolwich; this is the Royal Garrison Church of St George, opposite the Royal Artillery Barracks, wrecked by a flying bomb in 1944. This church is now run by a trust of dedicated volunteers who open the building to the public at weekends, when one can also visit the remains of the boiler house which still has a supply of 1944 coal on hand!

Right A garden has been created inside the walls of the bombed-out Christ Church, Newgate, close to St Paul's.

V-FOR-VICTORY TILING

During the dark days of the Blitz, something of a tradition built up amongst the East End's roofers by repairing bomb blasted tiles with a 'V for Victory' pattern in repaired roofs, with different coloured tiles to show the message. Sometimes, it was just a letter 'V', but at other locations was slightly more intricate; for example, a 'V' followed by the Morse code equivalent for the letter. Nowadays, very few examples survive but one can be clearly seen on the roof of The Cricketers pub at Woodford Green.

Above The 'V-for-Victory' tiling on The Cricketers Pub, Woodford Green, created by roofers who repaired the tiles after bomb damage.

MEMORIAL TO FIRST BOMB ON CITY OF LONDON

While not a scar of the Blitz as such, this memorial stone marks the spot where the first bomb fell on the City of London during the early hours of 25 August 1940. However, this was not the first bomb to fall on Greater London, but simply the first to fall within the city's Square Mile. It can be found at Fore Street in The Barbican. Less poignant than the tangible wounds left behind from bombing attacks, it is nevertheless a part of London's 'Blitz Legacy', just like the memorial plaque in Farringdon Road (see page 11) which marks where a building was destroyed in a Zeppelin raid during the First World War.

ON THIS SITE AT 12·15 A·M ON THE 25TH AUGUST 1940 FELL THE FIRST BOMB ON THE CITY OF LONDON IN THE SECOND WORLD WAR

Above The memorial stone marking the spot where the first bomb fell in the City's square mile.
Top Encapsulated in this one section of London's bomb damage maps, the extent of destruction during the Blitz can be seen. This area is centred on St Paul's Cathedral, showing how close to destruction the iconic building at the heart of London came.

EWS SIGNAGE

Emergency Water Supply signs can be found in various locations. These supplies were established when it became clear that conventional mains supplies were vulnerable to damage and were located at strategic points in cofferdams or basements of bombed-out buildings. The signs denoted the location and amount of water stored.

Above The painted Emergency Water Supply at St Paul's School remains in reasonably good condition after 80 years exposure to the elements.

INCENDIARY BOMB DAMAGE

Rather scarcer is evidence of incendiary bomb damage, but it can be seen at two locations in London. The interior of St Margaret's Church, opposite the Houses of Parliament, contains a charred pew and a damaged stained-glass window, which is the legacy of an oil bomb dropped on 25 September 1940. In the City of London, the Memorial to Heroic Self Sacrifice at Postman's Park also contains charred timber, this time from an incendiary bomb dropped on 29 December 1940. The bomb lodged in the roof tiles but was dealt with by a passing AFS crew.

Above These wooden beams to shelter roofing for the Memorial to Heroic Self Sacrifice at London's Postman's Park look to be painted black. In fact, they were scorched black by an incendiary bomb.

The Grim Toll

When the ordinary people of Britain were placed in the 'Front Line' between 1939 and 1945, the scale of destruction and loss of life resulting from German attacks was truly grievous.

Within the first few weeks of the Second World War, the civilian population of the British Isles found itself under German assault. It was a danger which persisted right up until the closing weeks of the war in 1945, the legacy of those attacks being felt long after the war's end through the deaths of family and friends at the enemy's hand, the destruction of property and, indeed, the loss of national architectural treasures.

As early as February 1941, the mounting scale of loss was such that the national government decided a record of those civilians killed should have a permanent status.

Consequently, a Royal Charter was established that same February which entrusted the role of listing these names to the Imperial War Graves Commission (now the Commonwealth War Graves Commission), it being ultimately decided that the names should be recorded in leather bound volumes and lodged in Westminster Abbey.

Today, that Roll is permanently displayed there under a perpetual light. Each day, a page is dutifully turned.

The Roll records the names of 60,595 civilians who died in attacks on Britain, with each individual lost being inscribed with their full name, age and date and place of death. This total includes 8,000 children.

By the end of September 1941, 42,000 people had lost their lives and this figure increased exponentially.

That tally, however, naturally rose and fell with the scale and tempo of German attacks, but it is sobering to note that around half of that early 42,000 death toll had died in the London Civil Defence Region as a result of the Blitz.

Left Rescue workers convey a casualty to an ambulance from a wrecked building during the Blitz. Given the clean and pristine condition of the uniforms and overalls, and the neat appearance of the rescuers, this is most likely a posed photograph to demonstrate the role of the rescue services.

Right Most certainly not posed is this image of dusty and dishevelled rescue workers including Police officers, ARP workers, civilians and a soldier taking a break in the aftermath of an air attack on a railway station. The state of the Police Sergeant's uniform with its ripped sleeve, and with his distant stare, tell their own grim story.

A DREADFUL AND TERRIFYING ORDEAL

The names embraced include commoner and Peers of the Realm alike, and from infants just hours old up to a centenarian Chelsea Pensioner. However, the total of 60,595 fatalities does not include British or Allied military personnel who died as the result of such attacks. In many cases, those personnel were caught up in attacks on civilian targets while they were off duty. In other instances, they were killed during attacks on military establishments.

Apart from the fatal casualties, an astonishing 86,182 civilians were injured sufficiently to need hospital admission while another 150,833 civilians were slightly injured. None of these statistics are perhaps surprising given that some 74,172 tons of high explosive (not including incendiary devices) were dropped on Britain by the Luftwaffe across the entire period of the war.

As to property and infrastructure, considerable damage was caused to industrial and commercial establishments with a large degree of disruption and dislocation to transport, communication

	Killed	Seriously Injured	Total
Bombing	51,509	61,423	112,932
Flying Bombs	6,148	17,981	24,165
Rockets	2,754	6,523	9,277
Cross-Channel Guns	148	255	403
Totals	**60,595**	**86,182**	**146,777**

Civilian casualties from bombing and various forms of long-range bombardment

Note: Of these 146,777 casualties, 80,397 (including about 90% of those caused by flying bombs and roughly the same proportion as those caused by rockets) occurred in the London Civil Defence Region, with 66,380 occurring elsewhere. The total number of civilians injured (that is, slightly injured plus those who were seriously injured) totalled 237,015.

Above In the immediate aftermath of an air raid, rescue workers toil among smouldering rubble and debris in a frantic search for survivors. More often-than-not, it was simply a grim task of recovering bodies. Scenes like these were repeated the length and breadth of Britain throughout the duration of the war.

'These cruel, wanton, indiscriminate bombings of London are, of course, a part of Hitler's invasion plans. He hopes, by killing large numbers of civilians, and women and children, that he will terrorise and cow the people of this mighty Imperial city. Little does he know the spirit of the British nation, or the tough fibre of the Londoners.'

Prime Minister, Winston S Churchill, September 1940.

networks and utilities. However, the scale of destruction to residential properties was immense. Two million homes were destroyed across Britain. In London alone 70,000 buildings were demolished, while an astonishing 1.7 million buildings in the city were damaged.

Also in the Capital, during the Blitz period, one in every six Londoners was rendered homeless at some point – 250,000 Londoners were displaced from their homes and many others rendered homeless in other towns and cities

Above Emblematic of Britain's ordeal and survival during the Blitz, this photograph of St Paul's Cathedral against a foreground of bombed and blazing building became one of the most famous photographs of the war. It was taken on the night of 29/30 December 1940. While the cathedral survived relatively unscathed, most of the buildings around it were razed to the ground.

For the whole of Britain's population, this had been a dreadful ordeal. Given the scale of loss, it is entirely appropriate that the lives of those who died remain commemorated in Westminster Abbey.

Those today who glibly use the term 'Blitz Spirit', sometimes associating that perceived quality with somewhat lesser catastrophes and events, should perhaps reflect soberly on the true awfulness of what the Blitz really meant to those who lived through it, endured it or were injured, killed or else made homeless because of it. ∎